Stop the Craziness:
Simple Life Solutions

Shirley B. Garrett, Psy.D

Stop the Craziness: Simple Life Solutions
Copyright © 2014 by Shirley B. Garrett, Psy.D.
All Rights Reserved.

No part of this publication may be reproduced, stored in a retrieval system, or transmitted in any way or by any means, electronic, mechanical, photocopy, recording, or otherwise, without the prior permission of the author except as provided by USA copyright law.

Book Design Copyright © 2014 by Shirley B. Garrett, Psy.D
Diva Pookie Boop Cartoons Copyright © 2014 by Shirley B. Garrett, Psy.D

Cover design by David W. Johnston

Published in the United States of America

ISBN-13: 978-0615974972

Revised in August, 2020

DEDICATION

This book is dedicated to all my former patients who over the many years trusted me with their secrets, emotional pain, and trauma. I did my best to guide them. They taught me so much and were the inspiration for this book. I hope the solutions these patients inspired will encourage and help others, thereby passing on their legacy of healing.

The stories in this book are composites of the thousands of cases I've worked over the many years of my counseling practice. Many of life's miseries are common among us all, even if we feel as if this only happened to us.
The names and circumstances have been altered to protect identities. I did this to preserve the confidentiality of my former patients. The examples used from my own life are true.

I applaud all my former patients for their endurance, courage, and perseverance. I watched many of you make the necessary changes to evolve into happier people. It was my privilege to serve you.

APPRECIATION

A special thanks to my parents, Margaret and Charlie Gunselman and my brother, Charles Gunselman. They loved me and led me to a career, that offered me an opportunity to make a difference in this world. My husband, Bob Garrett, deserves my gratitude for his love, support, patience, and his proof-reading from a left-brained perspective. He was also my technical guru, who rescued me on many occasions. Thanks to Ann and Henry Garrett for raising such a wonderful son and their support of my writing.

I had a number of editors who added quality to this book. Jennifer Lee Spain proofed and offered that valuable young adult perspective. Kathy Rhodes gave me helpful input regarding structure. Barbara Higgins, MA, LPC was not only a diligent proof-reader, but kept me on track from the counseling perspective.

I also received help and guidance from several writers groups; the Huntsville Literary Association (HLA) and the former Coffee Tree Books & Brew Writers.

I would like to thank David Johnston for his creativity and patience while designing the book cover.

Last, but not least, I offer affection and appreciation to my bibliocat, Pookie, who lounged on my desk while I wrote. She was the inspiration for the original Diva Pookie Boop cartoons in this book.

Table of Contents

- WHAT IS THE BLACK HOLE? 8
- SOLUTION 1: DO THE RIGHT THING 17
- SOLUTION 2: THE WORLD DOESN'T REVOLVE AROUND YOU 23
- SOLUTION 3: SPEND YOUR TIME ON THINGS THAT MATTER 29
- SOLUTION 4: WHAT GOES AROUND COMES AROUND 33
- SOLUTION 5: WHAT YOU DO, HAS AN IMPACT ON THE WORLD 37
- SOLUTION 6: FOCUS PROVIDES THE FUEL 41
- SOLUTION 7: AVOID BECOMING A NEGATIVITY MAGNET 45
- SOLUTION 8: BE A BALLOON, NOT A BRICK 49
- SOLUTION 9: POWER, CONTROL, AND RESPONSIBILITY 55
- SOLUTION 10: ACCEPT - LEARN - AVOID REPETITION 59
- SOLUTION 11: EVERY TIME YOU REPEAT A MISTAKE, THE CONSEQUENCES GET WORSE 63
- SOLUTION 12: "THE PLATINUM RULE" 67
- SOLUTION 13: GARBAGE IN = GARBAGE OUT 71
- SOLUTION 14: LIFE IS LIKE A GARDEN 77
- SOLUTION 15: BE NICE TO YOURSELF 81
- SOLUTION 16: PLAY BY THE RULES 85
- SOLUTION 17: RESPECT YOURSELF 89
- SOLUTION 18: RESPECT OTHERS 93
- SOLUTION 19: LIFE IS A PROCESS 97
- SOLUTION 20: YOUR TIME IS PRICELESS 103
- SOLUTION 21: LISTEN 107
- SOLUTION 22: JUST BECAUSE YOUR FRIENDS DO IT 111
- SOLUTION 23: WRITE DOWN YOUR GOALS 115
- SOLUTION 24: BREAK GOALS INTO SMALL PARTS CALLED OBJECTIVES 119
- SOLUTION 25: UNDERSTAND YOUR GENETICS 123

SOLUTION 26: "IT IS EASIER TO AVOID TEMPTATION THAN TO RESIST IT." 127

SOLUTION 27: AVOID THE ATTITUDE OF ENTITLEMENT 131

SOLUTION 28: ATTITUDE OF GRATITUDE 136

SOLUTION 29: GUARD YOUR ATTITUDE 140

SOLUTION 30: AVOID GOSSIP 144

SOLUTION 31: DON'T TAUNT OR BE UNKIND TO OTHERS 148

SOLUTION 32: FIND SOMETHING POSITIVE IN EVERY SITUATION 152

SOLUTION 33: HOPE FOR A GOOD OUTCOME, BUT TAKE REASONABLE PRECAUTIONS 156

SOLUTION 34: HAVE PLAN "A", PLAN "B" AND PLAN "C" 160

SOLUTION 35: "THIS TOO SHALL PASS" 164

SOLUTION 36: CHANGE IS INEVITABLE 168

SOLUTION 37: AVOID PRIMARY AND SECONDARY ABUSE 172

SOLUTION 38: TAKE OUT YOUR PERSONAL GARBAGE 178

SOLUTION 39: USE FORGIVENESS AS YOUR SHOVEL 182

SOLUTION 40: WORRY LESS AND ACT MORE 186

SOLUTION 41: HAVE GOOD BOUNDARIES 190

SOLUTION 42: "NO" IS A POSITIVE WORD 194

SOLUTION 43: YOU CAN DETACH IN A LOVING WAY 199

SOLUTION 44: BALANCE, BALANCE, BALANCE 203

SOLUTION 45: BE A THERMOSTAT, NOT A THERMOMETER 207

SOLUTION 46: CONTROL YOUR MOUTH 211

SOLUTION 47: LOVE MORE–FEAR LESS 215

SOLUTION 48: PRACTICE TOLERANCE 219

SOLUTION 49: RECREATE YOURSELF 223

SOLUTION 50: THE BEGINNING! 227

Diva Pookie Boop

What is the Black Hole?

Do you experience more than your share of hardships? Have you given up on happiness? Is life a series of ruined relationships? Do you want your life to be different—better? There are solutions, so don't give up hope.

Jane learned how to improve her life and so can you. Jane perched on the sofa in my therapy office, as tears poured down her face. She reached for another tissue, blotting the mascara smudged under her eyes.

"I really thought this guy was different."

In her efforts to avoid being alone, Jane once again picked the wrong guy. He, like the ones before him, broke her heart.

"This guy seemed like such an improvement over the last guy I dated."

Indeed, he was, because he didn't hit her or drink himself into a stupor every night. However, he was unfaithful and deceived her. Jane took a deep shuddering breath and said, "Boy, I can really pick them."

> **Every decision you make or path you choose has the potential to change your life.**

Jane was circling a Black Hole. She repeated the same dysfunctional pattern of her parents' marriage. Her father, an abusive alcoholic, was involved in a number of affairs. Her mother stayed in the marriage out of fear and a warped sense of security. This was the pattern Jane saw growing up; it was what she knew. She thought it was normal. The only difference was Jane avoided marriage as a solution to side-step an unhappy one. Unfortunately, she didn't evade the emotional pain, because she repeatedly picked men who were similar to her father. Through therapy, she realized her chances of finding her ideal mate were lower when she searched for romance in a bar. Jane eventually chose to *Stop the Craziness* in her life that made her unhappy. She applied many of the simple life solutions in this book, to pick a good man and to develop a healthy relationship. She created a happier life and you can, too.

> **Beat the odds – don't be a statistic.**

> **To understand how you fell into a hole doesn't help you climb out of it. However, it may keep you from falling in the same hole again.**

Every decision you make or path you choose has the potential to change your life and can lead to life-long consequences of a positive or negative nature. Be honest with yourself: Are you repeating mistakes and entrenching yourself in negative patterns? If so, this book may change your life. Beat the odds—don't be a statistic.

In the twenty-six years I've worked as a counselor, I've seen countless clients of all ages suffer due to the repetition of negative behavior patterns. Some, like Jane, were unable to see the pattern. The entire situation was too close for her to have a clear perspective. It would be like trying to read this book with it pressed against your nose, too close. If you hold the book some distance away, you're able to see the words and understand the content. Jane needed an objective viewpoint to be able to see her life situation. She also needed a historical perspective to identify the patterns in her life.

Jane lived her life based on the faulty family beliefs and misinformation she learned as a child. She modeled her behavior after her parents, who in her case, didn't have a clue about happy, healthy relationships. Both Jane and her parents were sliding down the Black Hole—a life of misery. To understand how you fell into a hole doesn't help you climb out of it. However, it may keep you from falling in the same hole again.

To blame the past only keeps you stuck in the Black Hole. It's time to *Stop the Craziness* and create your new life now. Take responsibility; learn the simple solutions of a happy life and suffer fewer negative consequences. Learn to love yourself. If that sentence frightened you, definitely keep reading this book.

Everyone should question their behavior and consider whether it's leading them toward a better life. Every decision, choice and action can move you in a positive, as well as a negative direction. Think about your family, school, employer, and community. How many people do you know who have experienced the following self-inflicted consequences due to just *ONE* unwise decision:

- An unplanned pregnancy, which resulted in teen parenthood, adoption, or an abortion,
- A sexually transmitted disease,
- Legal problems,
- Alcohol addiction,
- Drug addiction,
- Physically scarred or injured for life,
- Death by an accident,
- Loss of employment,
- Bankruptcy,

- Divorce or loss of relationships.

None of these people thought something like this would ever happen to them. While you may feel you are lucky, powerful, clever, and smart, you are just as vulnerable to life-altering consequences as the rest of the human race.

It has happened to all of us. We made a poor choice and started the cycle of misery, spiraling into the Black Hole. Then the craziness starts. We each have to find our way out of the repeated cycle of poor choices and self-sabotaging behaviors.

> **It is not always clear when you start a path, where it may lead.**

Please don't think you are the only one who has made mistakes. Mistakes are part of the learning process. It's impossible to avoid *all* mistakes. It is possible to make good decisions and avoid *many* painful mistakes. It's not always clear when you start a path, where it may lead.

To flourish in the world and achieve your desires, you must first know how to work with the system of life in an ethical way. Life has a system and a set of rules that can help you reach your goals, be happy, and to create the life you desire. When you know and follow these simple solutions, you will enjoy the world with fewer problems and more rewards. You can create the life of your dreams.

Life is like a video game. Every game has rules and levels of achievement. The wise player learns the rules, remembers the previous moves to avoid pitfalls, and chooses the safest path through the levels. This is how higher scores are achieved. It takes most adults years to acquire the knowledge of how the world works, and an unfortunate few never do.

I chose the title of this chapter after hearing many of my patients describe their lives as a "Black Hole." In Space, a Black Hole is defined as a region of spacetime, from which gravity prevents anything, including light, from escaping. It sucks you in and consumes you. It sounds like something from a nightmare doesn't it. Your situation isn't a real Black Hole, so it's possible to escape.

When life leaves you feeling empty instead of abundant, it is time to do something different. *Stop the Craziness*, create a happy life, and work toward your dreams. Over the past twenty-six years, many of my patients have successfully used the real-life solutions in this book.

I want you to imagine that I'm speaking to you as your friend. A friend who is willing to tell you what you need to hear to improve your life. These fifty simple solutions will transform your life *if you use them*. Think of them as the uncommon, common sense. They are simple and easy to apply. However, they only work if you use them. Some of the solutions only take minutes a day. These solutions will help you *Stop the Craziness* and the downward spiral into the Black Hole. Why keep making the same painful mistakes, if you can learn a better system to life? I'm not saying this book will keep you from making *any* mistakes.

Don't be afraid that you may not be able to do this. If you were successful at making a mess of your life, you can successfully transform your life to a positive state. I'ts just a different approach.

Of course the earlier in life that you start, the easier it will be. Teenagers for example, are at a critical age, because they are on the edge of adulthood. Many of their consequences can affect their life as an adult.

I won't beat you over the head with your problems like so many books, which then offer only a few suggestions at the end. If you are like most of us, you do that to yourself already with zero results.

This is a solution-focused book. It doesn't replace the therapy process; it is only one of the many tools available to you to improve your insight and personal growth. I do hope it inspires you to become your best self.

I designed the book to help adults, young adults, and teens to *Stop the Craziness* and transform their worlds, in order to live a more satisfying life.

There is a "Positive Direction Intervention" at the end of each chapter for the readers who are sick and tired of spinning in the craziness of the Black Hole and desire to escape NOW! To reach the maximum effect, it's necessary to do the Positive Direction Interventions in each chapter. As you read these simple solutions and apply the Positive Direction Interventions, you may find you are already doing some of these positive things. Good for you – that's less for you to change. Keep in mind, knowing the information and using the information are two different things altogether. There may be information in this book you never knew. You may read information you know, but forgot or haven't used. Knowledge only has power if you use it wisely.

I'm not asking you to change who you are. I'm asking you to evolve into your best self.

I "double-dog dare you" to use this book to *Stop the Craziness* and recreate your life. I know you can do it, because I did.

Positive Direction Intervention

List 3 habits that you are *willing* to change in order to have a happier life. They can be small changes, because small steps can lead to big results. For example, "I will get up ten minutes earlier, so I won't have to rush. This will reduce my stress level."

1.
2.
3.

Inspirational Thought

Diva Pookie Boop

Stop the Craziness: Simple Life Solutions

Diva Pookie Boop

Solution 1: Do the Right Thing

Three simple transformational guidelines, which can drastically reduce the number of negative consequences that could cost you time, happiness, freedom, and money, are:

- Do the *RIGHT THING*;
- Do it for the *RIGHT REASONS*;
- Do it the *RIGHT WAY*.

Follow this formula and your life will stay on a more positive track. The fewer negative consequences you encounter the happier you will be. The *RIGHT THING* guideline, requires that you know right from wrong. Highly dysfunctional families sometimes teach a skewed version of morality. Morals are the internalized rules by which we live our lives. A simple gauge to follow is:

- If the behavior will get you in trouble, avoid it.
- Will you or your family be mortified or proud if your actions are the leading story on the evening news?
- If your conscience made you squirm, it's probably not the right thing to do.

Perhaps it would be wise to take a minute to think about and write down your moral code. It will be easier for you to do the *RIGHT THING*, if you're clear about your morals. A plan of action usually increases your chances for a peak performance and outcome. If you feel stuck, don't be upset; some people have difficulty with this task. Think about the things that you wouldn't want people to do to you such as lie, cheat, steal, or gossip about you. If you wouldn't want something done to you, then it is a good idea to avoid doing it to others. Some people use the Ten Commandments as a guideline. The do the *RIGHT THING* principle is important because when you create negativity in any form, it bounces back to you.

Positive Direction Intervention

Write out your moral code

1.
2.
3.
4.
5.
6.
7.
8.
9.
10.

John was double smart, street smart, and book smart. Funding a college education became John's primary goal during his senior year of high school. He qualified for student loans, but preferred an easier route. Being bilingual, John misused his talent for languages and began trafficking drugs between Mexico and the United States. He intended to cease his criminal activity after he graduated and found a job. The authorities arrested him at the end of his senior year in college, and he nearly lost everything. To avoid jail, he provided information about others in the drug operation, which placed his life in jeopardy. John received probation for two years and he now has a felony charge on his record. After his family and friends discovered his illegal secret, John found it necessary to move to a different area of the country to escape his notoriety and for his safety.

> **You can escape many things, but never yourself.**

John told me, "I knew what I was doing was wrong, I just thought I could get away with it long enough to finish college and no one would ever know."

I asked, "Do you ever think about the harm inflicted by the drugs you trafficked into the United States?"

John hung his head. "Everyday. A friend's brother recently died of a drug overdose. I know the drugs I smuggled are long gone, but I can't help but wonder, how many people overdosed or ruined their lives because of me."

It's important that you think about how your actions affect you personally and the world around you, not just for the moment, but also in the future. Living with guilt the way John does, can create destructive unhappiness.

The second guideline, do it for the *RIGHT REASONS*, requires pure motives. Humans make daily choices based on a multitude of motives, some altruistic and positive, others are self-serving. Your primary motives need to be good ones. It may seem unimportant, but you will go to bed every night feeling better about yourself as a person. Being able to love yourself is important for personal happiness. You can escape many things, but never yourself.

The third guideline is to do no harm by doing things the *RIGHT WAY*. No harm means not hurting other people or the environment. Also, it means avoiding damage to your own character or body. Harmful actions may speed along the results you desire, but later can neutralize a good outcome.

James wanted to be buff, but was unwilling to do it the *RIGHT WAY*. A friend at the gym told him about steroids and he decided to try them. He had a vague recollection about side effects but didn't investigate them. He became more irritable and aggressive and this caused problems with his wife, who couldn't understand nor tolerate his behavior. After losing his temper and hitting her, she left him. Short-term consequences for James were the loss of his marriage and half of his assets. Long-term, he developed cancer and lost his health, as well as his hard-earned muscles.

An easy solution may not be the best solution. James chose a quick solution to reach his goal. It ruined his life and nearly killed him.

Make the right choices, even if you receive pressure from others to do the wrong things. James received a great deal of pressure to try the steroids and then became hooked on the quick results. It's not easy to make the right choices, but it's im-portant that you do it anyway.

An easy solution may not be the best solution.

Someone will always be displeased with your decisions. What pleases one person will displease another, but you are the one who must live with your consequences. The ultimate payoff for following these guidelines is worth the effort. You can hold your head high and feel better about yourself. You can change your friends, go to a different school, or change employment, but it's impossible to escape yourself. You know from experience, you are your own worst critic.

Therefore, do the *RIGHT THING*, for the *RIGHT REASONS*, the *RIGHT WAY* to increase your joy and avoid many of life's negative consequences.

Positive Direction Intervention

Think of a situation in your life and apply it now.

1. The right thing to do is...
2. The right reason is...
3. The right way to approach the situation is...

These are three simple guidelines, which are easy to use. If you don't use the "Positive Direction Interventions" in this book, they can't help you to transform your life. It is important to write things down when requested, to help make them clear in your mind. The interventions are important, simple and don't take much time. If you avoid doing them, you will dilute your progress.

Diva Pookie Boop

Solution 2: The World Doesn't Revolve Around You

In normal family life, it is necessary for infants and young children to be the center of attention and care.

However, parents must wean their children from the attitude of entitlement, as they get older. There is a difference between needs and desires. Providing every desire of your children, instead of gradually training them to take on more responsibility, is a formula for heartache in the future. Overindulgence will handicap your children. Adults and teens that suffer from the attitude of entitlement, have much frustration and unhappiness.

You may identify with either the adult or teen in the following scenario.

Marsha's flushed face contorted with anger. She paced the floor in front of the sofa as she shared her dilemma. Zack, her seventeen year-old son left an inpatient program for alcohol and drug abuse against professional advice. He then came home and stole her checkbook. He forged checks on her account, which exceeded her balance. She now had five overdrawn checks.

> **Overindulgence will handicap your children.**

Marsha had a long history of search-and-rescue efforts with Zack. I suggested she file juvenile charges to provide consequences. I explained it was better to let him experience the cost of criminal behavior as a juvenile, because juvenile records are sealed at adulthood. I also told her the judge would place her son on a curfew and his juvenile probation officer would require regular drug screens. She stopped her pacing and glared at me.

"I can't do that to my child!" She crossed her arms and narrowed her eyes.

I next suggested she have him pay back what he stole, as well as the bounced check charges. She placed her hands on her hips and looked at me as if I were daft.

"He doesn't have a job. He can't do that."

There was no reason Zack couldn't get a job, except he couldn't pass a drug screen. My final suggestion was to work off his payments through household chores.

Marsha folded her arms back across her chest. "He doesn't do chores. He'll get mad if I ask him to do chores."

"Zack needs to understand that he isn't the center of the universe and that consequences apply to him, just like everyone else," I explained.

"Zach is the center of *my world* and I won't let him suffer in *any way,* if I can help it."

It was clear who was in charge in this family, and it wasn't Marsha. Marsha chose the path of least resistance, without considering the future costs. She was saving Zack from everything, except himself. She required nothing from Zack. She paid off the bounced checks and return check charges.

She stole her son's consequences, and therefore, his opportunity to learn. She was a lesson thief.

Three years later, Marsha was back in my office, clutching my throw pillow to her chest. She blurted out with one breath, "I'm not sleeping, I worry all the time, and I may have to file bankruptcy."

For the past three years, Marsha had been circling the Black Hole with Zack. She was in a repeat cycle of uncompleted treatment programs, stolen checks, bounced check charges, and most recently, Zack stole her credit card.

Marsha's failure to provide consequences to her son, led him to the erroneous conclusion, that there are no negative consequences for bad behavior. Mom will always make them go away. This was because she didn't teach Zack he wasn't the center of the solar system. She never dispelled his beliefs of entitlement. Her son, as an adult was repeating the same behaviors of his years as a teen, but now Marsha was trying to save him from adult consequences. I offered numerous suggestions, which Marsha declined. Marsha would do anything to avoid conflict with her son, even if conflict and consequences might help her son in the future. My greatest fear was that Zack would die someday from an overdose or other drug related mishap, because she wasn't willing to let him suffer consequences.

> **The attitude of entitlement will make you a prisoner in your own life.**

A message for the teen readers: if your parents don't require you to have responsibilities around your home, they are cheating you out of valuable discipline and training opportunities. This will deny you skills you will need later in life. Going into the world on your own will be both exciting and frightening. The more life skills you acquire and the more self-discipline you possess, the more confident you will be. If your parents are paying for every little thing you want, they are conditioning you for disappointment. When you are an adult, you will have difficulty adjusting to financial reality, and as a result, you may find yourself deeply in debt. Debt is negative energy that will pull you deeper into the Black Hole.

If you are an adult and your parents are *still paying* your bills, it is time for a change. It's difficult to feel powerful as an adult when you're financially dependent on others.

There will always be rules in your life, no matter your age. School systems and employers have their own sets of rules, just like your family. To cope and be content, you will sometimes have to accept that some things are beyond your control.

To transform your life it is important to understand you are a small part of the universe, not the center of it. The attitude of entitlement will make you a prisoner in your own life. Positive, emotionally healthy people are repelled by a negative self-centered attitude.

Positive Direction Intervention

List three things that are out of your control that you are willing to learn to accept. Write them down.

1.

2.

3.

Inspirational Thought

Don't be discouraged. Your life is your play and only you have the power to rewrite your life script. You write it everyday of your life.

Diva Pookie Boop

Diva Pookie Boop

Solution 3: Spend Your Time on Things That Matter

How much effort are you willing to put forth to get what you want? How important is it to you?

You make decisions regarding the degree of time, money, and effort you choose to allot to the daily dealings of your life. Don't waste time trying to control things that aren't important to you or are out of your control. There are things that you will need to maintain for prosperity, health, and safety reasons, such as study to achieve a degree, good personal hygiene, and maintenance for your car. In general, proceed by the *good enough* principle, wisely using the realities of where you live, work, and go to school. Save your best efforts toward excellence, for areas of life where it is important.

> **Save your best efforts toward excellence, for areas of life where it is important.**

In other words, it is a waste of time to spend an hour polishing the wood dining table when ten minutes is sufficient. My mother who had Obsessive Compulsive Disorder (OCD) wasted much of her life doing unimportant things to perfection. It's just as unproductive to obsess over changing clothing syles or other things that will change in a blink of an eye.

However, it's not a waste of time to spend an hour updating your resume for an employment opportunity.

Your very future may be at stake. Any action that improves you emotionally, physically or mentally is a good investment of your time.

Just as you have to follow an employer's personnel policy at work or the rules at school, you must also follow the rules when you live in another person's home. This is worth your time and effort. It's important to respect their property and their decisions about what is important to them.

When you move out on your own and pay your own bills, you earn the right to gain more control over your life, how you spend your time, and determine how other people treat your home.

If you are married or have a roommate, it is important to come to an agreement about the household rules and respect them. Irreparable damage to a friendship or marriage can occur due to this form of disrespect. This leads to unhappiness.

An acquaintance of mine, named Chuck, was famous for his lazy and passive-aggressive behavior. He was an attractive and amicable man who worked harder at avoiding work than completing a task. He spent his time on television, video games and surfing the Internet, while avoiding his responsibilities at home. He didn't spend his time wisely. Through his passive-aggressive behaviors, Chuck had managed to shirk almost all of his chores at home. He just wouldn't do them, offering numerous excuses. He learned from experience that if he made things frustrating or inconvenient enough, Marian, his wife, would eventually take on the additional responsibility.

Marian worked outside the home and juggled all the home duties, except the disposal of the garbage. With tenacity, she insisted that her husband perform this one task. Chuck used every excuse and option to assure each week that there would be a battle over the garbage.

What Chuck didn't realize was that this minor task had come to symbolize his lack of participation in the marriage. All her mounting resentments and disappointments focused like a laser beam, on his behavior regarding the garbage.

One day, Marian gathered the garbage and placed the large bag in front of the door that Chuck must exit to go to his car. She watched with arms folded, as Chuck slid the bag over with his foot, so he could open the door, then he stepped over the bag and left for work. Marian filed for divorce, and received half of all the assets, plus alimony.

What is *not* important to you, may be *extremely* important to the people who share your life. Spend your time on what is important to you, but keep in mind the things that are important to the significant people in your life. To be responsible for your life gives you control and more ability to transform your life to the one you desire. Focus your time and assets toward the areas most important to you and your well-being.

Positive Direction Intervention

List three areas where it would be important for you to focus your time.

1.

2.

3.

Stop the Craziness: Simple Life Solutions | 31

Diva Pookie Boop

Solution 4: What Goes Around Comes Around

Behavior and consequences. Some religions call this karma, some people call it justice, and others say, "You reap what you sow." You receive consequences for *all* your actions and behaviors, both *positive* and *negative*. You will receive a consequence for your actions, even if you aren't caught.

Doug sat on the edge of my sofa and repeatedly ran his hand through his hair. He was worried about his daughter, whose schoolmates were taunting her. They called her "skinny" and "four-eyes." He felt helpless to stop the verbal abuse, which made his daughter cry on a daily basis.

"You know Doc, this has really made me think about all those kids I bullied in elementary school. I remember this one skinny kid in my class who wore glasses. I terrorized that kid. My friends and I would grab his glasses and throw them to each other over his head, while we taunted him. I actually felt powerful every time I watched that kid cringe. I can't even remember his name, because we just called him 'Four Eyes'. I wonder how many times he went home and cried to his parents. I thought calling him names was funny then, I don't think it's funny now."

Doug didn't pay for his bad behavior immediately, but he was certainly suffering many years later by watching his daughter's agony. It gave him a different perspective on his actions.

Stop the Craziness: Simple Life Solutions

Sometimes consequences are immediate. Many of my patients were arrested due to driving while intoxicated. The arrest was an immediate consequence. Later when they went to court, they lost their license, paid a monetary fine, were required to attend a treatment program, and their car insurance rate skyrocketed. These were delayed, long-term consequences. Of course, this made their lives unhappy and miserable.

> **You decide your own fate by what you choose to do.**

You never get away with anything, not really. Think about possible consequences for your decisions, both immediate and long-term, before you act. While poor choices can set you up for painful lessons, good choices set you up for wonderful things to happen in your life.

This is powerful information! You create a happier life through good, well thought out decisions. If you want control over your life, you can't blame your consequences, good or bad, on anyone but yourself. Other than the family you were born into and your genetics, you pretty much decide your own fate by what you choose to do. Think immediate and long-term.

Positive Direction Intervention

Write one behavior that you are willing to change today that will save you from negative consequences. List the steps to make that change. Remember small steps can transform your life.

Inspirational Thought

Diva Pookie Boop

Stop the Craziness: Simple Life Solutions

Diva Pookie Boop

Solution 5: What You Do, has an Impact on the World

You don't live in a vacuum; you live in the world. The world is like a large pond. If you throw a rock into the middle of the pond, the ripples are the most intense at the place the rock entered the water, and they gradually decrease in intensity as the ripples move toward the shore. That one rock disturbed the whole pond.

> **Every decision or choice you make in life may have consequences that affect you and everyone involved with you for years into the future.**

Similarly, when you take a positive or negative action, the people closest to you are the most intensely affected, but the consequences of your behavior can spread to your family, friends, community or even the world. Every de-cision or choice you make in life may have consequences that affect you and everyone involved with you for years into the future.

One simple choice can lead to the next event, which leads to the next event, like a chain of dominoes, tipping over each domino, until they all fall.

In 2007, I was poisoned. Poor quality control of a liquid vitamin, resulted in the poisoning of me and over 700 other people by overdoses of selenium and chromium. Both of these trace elements are required for good health, but in large amounts can kill. One careless action by a person(s) caused hundreds of people across the nation to be ill, lose hair, nails, and to deal with a lifetime of physical complications. This issue of poor quality control also affected families, friends, healthcare establishments, insurance companies, employers, and the legal system. One mistake created a huge, costly impact. Fortunately, there were no deaths.

Think of all the people affected by one decision made by one person—YOU. A small positive action toward just one person, like a smile, could spread around the world. Your actions make a difference in the world; make sure your effect is one you can look back on with pride, not regret.

Positive Direction Intervention

Write down three small things that you have done to create a positive impact on just one person in the last week.

1.

2.

3.

Inspirational Thought

Diva Pookie Boop

Diva Pookie Boop

Solution 6: Focus Provides the Fuel

You are the taskmaster; you are in charge. Every day you unknowingly tell your unconscious mind where to concentrate the focus of your life by your thoughts, emotions, and attention. You play a part in creating your life. Whatever you give your focus and attention, it creates power in your life.

> **Attention and focus are powerful forces – as powerful as directing the sun through a magnifying glass.**

If you make school your target, it will become important to you and your grades will improve. You will move up in academic standing and be able to enter the college, trade school, or graduate program of your choice. If your efforts center to-ward your career, you will have more success in this area of your life. If you concentrate on the relationships you have with important people in your life, they will become deeper and more fulfilling. If you are single-minded toward spiritual growth, you will become centered and closer to God.

Jamie put his focus and effort toward acquiring alcohol and drugs. The need for the chemically-induced high took over his life and consumed him. He made his decisions and choices

> **Whatever you give your focus and attention creates power in your life.**

with addictive substances in mind. As a result, he lost his

employment, his wife divorced him, and he lost custody of his son. Jamie is now serving time for numerous drug-related charges. He told me, "All I could think about was my next high, and how I was going to get it."

Attention and focus are powerful forces, as powerful as directing the sun through a magnifying glass. Just like the magnifying glass, the more intense the focus the faster things ignite.

Religious leaders tell us God guides everything in our lives. God also gave us *free will.* Keep in mind that humans can *free will* ourselves into many negative consequences, that result in heartache for ourselves and others.

Since the unconscious is an efficient taskmaster, you must be careful to center your attention in a positive way, one that will give you the life you desire. Where have you been focusing your attention? Is it working for you?

Positive Direction Intervention

1. Pick one area in your life that you can focus on to improve. Write it down.
2. Take just one small step in the right direction each day for the next week.

Inspirational Thought

Just as there are different ways to cross an ocean, there are different ways to solve a problem. Think of all the possible options before determining your course of action

Diva Pookie Boop

Diva Pookie Boop

Solution 7: Avoid Becoming a Negativity Magnet

The unconscious is the deeper part of our minds that operates without our awareness. Without knowing it, our feelings, thoughts, desires or beliefs can surface from the unconscious, and drive our behaviors. Have you ever driven to work and didn't remember the trip? That was your unconscious mind, driving.

You tell your unconscious what to focus on, and guide you toward, by giving your attention to those things. If you tell yourself and others you attract jerks, then you're telling your unconscious to find more jerks to hurt you. If you focus on the negative, you will become a negativity magnet. The unconscious follows clear orders in a competent fashion.

Direct your unconscious to find helpful and supportive people to guide you toward your goals. Seek out and learn from the people who have accomplished their dreams. Concentrate on your goals and seek mentors to help you accomplish them. Attract positive people.

> **Seek out and learn from the people who have accomplished their dreams.**

Susan knew for years that she wanted to be a veterinarian. She was at the point in life where she was free to pursue this goal. Susan was smart. She laid the foundation for this goal for a year. She had volunteered her time at both the Humane Society and at a local vet. Her vet became her mentor and taught her many valuable lessons about the clinical and business side of veterinary practice. She even wrote letters of recommendation on Susan's behalf. Susan was so focused on her goal, she found herself doing unconscious things that helped her reach her goal. She is currently attending the school of her choice. It wouldn't surprise anyone if Susan graduated and eventually became a partner in her mentor's practice. She was a positivity magnet.

Mentors are available in every profession and most of them feel complimented if asked to share their wisdom.

Remember, your mentor's time is valuable, so use it wisely.

Attract positive people and situations and your life is likely to be abundant with joy. Attract negative people to you, and you will suffer and be miserable. Go for the joy in life. Why suffer unnecessarily? You can't be happy by surrounding yourself with negativity.

Positive Direction Intervention

1. Think of several people whom you would consider to be future mentors. Write down their names now.

2. Contact one to discuss your future and ask if he or she would be your mentor. If not, ask the next one on your list. In order to get what you want; you have to be willing to ask.

Inspirational Thought

Diva Pookie Boop

Stop the Craziness: Simple Life Solutions

Diva Pookie Boop

Solution 8: Be a Balloon, Not a Brick

Are you similar to a balloon that soars high with optimism and hope? Do you have lofty goals?

Are you more like a brick that is heavy, earthbound, and stuck in the mud with negative thoughts and destructive behaviors?

Are your friend's bricks or balloons? My grandmother preached the old English proverb, "Birds of a feather flock together." Research indicates that people tend to congregate with others who are in a comparable social class, share similar beliefs, or have the same hobbies.

Two or more people with positive attitudes create more positive energy than one.

If you take balloons and tie them together, each of them offer lift to the others. Together, they soar higher and at a faster rate of speed. A single balloon has the lift capacity of one balloon. Two balloons together, have the lift capacity of three balloons. The same is true for people. Two or more people with positive attitudes create more positive energy than one.

Are your friends healthy, happy, responsible, and have goals for their lives? Are they helping you reach your goals? Are they balloons, ready to help lift you to the happiness and fulfillment you desire?

Bricks are people who *choose* to be negative, critical, and gossipy. They typically indulge in self-sabotaging behaviors, and have no plans for their future. A few don't care who they harm. They are stuck in the mud of their own negativity and bad habits.

If you tie a balloon to a brick, the balloon will valiantly try to lift the brick, but the brick will hold the balloon down. Eventually the balloon will lose its buoyancy and deflate. It will sink into the mud with the brick.

> **Balloons can't make a brick fly.**
> **Bricks don't fly.**

Balloons can't make a brick fly. Bricks don't fly.

The brick must *choose* to become a balloon and take the steps to transform. Make the choice to be a balloon and choose to fly.

Encourage bricks by the beauty of your flight and your positive choices and behaviors. Don't tie yourself to a brick.

If you have attached yourself to a brick, consider a responsible way to detach. Beware; bricks don't like to lose their balloons, so manipulation may be used to keep you. Bricks often use fear, control, guilt, and may even threaten harm to you, your family, pets or themselves. Years ago I did a mental health consult. The young male I was to evaluate had taken a full bottle of Tylenol as a suicide gesture in an attempt to keep his estranged girlfriend as an emotional hostage. She had finally left him after years of addiction and abuse. He told me, "I didn't want to take anything really bad that might hurt me. I thought I would swallow the bottle of pills and call her, so she could take me to the ER. I figured she would feel so bad, that she would come home." People often attempt suicide with this

> **Encourage bricks by the beauty of your flight and your positive choices and behaviors. Don't tie yourself to a brick.**

over-the-counter medication, assuming it won't really hurt or kill them. That's a deadly assumption.

What he didn't know was that an overdose of Tylenol could kill his liver.

His girlfriend avoided his calls because he had phoned her excessively during a twenty-four hours period. Consequently, hours passed before she accepted a call. Meanwhile, the critical period passed to pump his stomach and the Tylenol was working its way through his system. The young man's attending physician explained that Tylenol poisoning has three phases. The person will feel sick the first day, and will feel much better the second day. By the end of the second or the third day, the liver will experience the full extent of the damage. This young man was likely to experience kidney failure, bleeding disorders, fall into a coma, and die.

I had the unsavory task, along with his physician, to inform him that he was likely to die within the next fourty-eight to seventy-two hours. A minister and an attorney were called to consult with the patient. His actions devastated his family. His physician transferred the young man by helicopter to a major hospital for treatment. I was not informed of the outcome. I prayed it was positive.

> **You are *not* responsible for another person's decisions or behaviors: You *are* responsible for yours.**

If a manipulative brick makes suicidal or homicidal threats to you, take it seriously. Contact 911 and a family member of that person. If the threats are a tactic to keep you hostage through fear and guilt, that person will be angry and embarrassed when the ambulance and police arrive. If the person is serious about those threats, an ambulance and police need to be present. Don't go there yourself. It may reinforce this exteme tactic. This could even be a setup for a murder-suicide. This type of situation requires the intervention of professionals.

Don't allow a brick to keep you as an emotional or financial hostage. You are *not* responsible for another person's decisions or behaviors. You *are* responsible for yours.

People will do exactly what they choose to do. Untie yourself, float free, and rise above all the bricks that want you to wallow in the mud.

Positive Direction Intervention

1. Decide if you want to be a brick or a balloon.

2. Determine who are the bricks in your life.

3. Decide who are the balloons in your life.

4. If you need help to untie yourself from a brick, seek guidance and support from a professional, who is wise to the wily ways of bricks.

Inspirational Thought

Diva Pookie Boop

Stop the Craziness: Simple Life Solutions

Diva Pookie Boop

Solution 9: Power, Control, and Responsibility

There are some basic rules of power, control, and responsibility.
1. If you are willing to be responsible and make good decisions, you will gain power, control, and privileges in your life. With this, your life could be more satisfying.
2. If you choose to be irresponsible, you will lose power, control, and privileges. Your life may be unhappy and less productive.

If you think you can have power, control, and privileges without being responsible, you are wrong, because for 99% of the world, it doesn't work that way. Think of responsibility as the *ability to respond* and to exert some control over your destiny. You want to have more control over your life, so you can create the life you desire. If you want to manage your life and maintain your privileges with your employer or parents, you must earn them by being responsible and following rules. Rules are the price of living in society. Rules protect all of us from ourselves.

> **Think of responsibility as the *ability to respond* and to exert some control over your destiny.**

Teens, when you are trustworthy, your parents will be willing to give you more freedom. Parents will exert less control over you if they feel they can trust your judgment.

Adults, the same is true of employers. When employers see trustworthy behaviors, less supervision is required. Therefore, if you don't want people micromanaging your life and work, show that you can be responsible. Keep in mind that trust takes time to establish and even longer to reestablish.

Imagine, you have reached the age of reason and you cast off in the river of life in your own little boat. You are now responsible for your own boat and its contents. You're floating along and suddenly things get rough. You reach for the oars but there are none. You look for a map of the river system to determine your destination, but there isn't one in your boat. In fact, your boat is devoid of any supplies. It is your boat, you made the choice to enter it, and you cast off into the river of life without the tools of survival. Who is responsible for this situation? You! Excuses such as, "If she hadn't… I wouldn't have…" or "He made me…" are just ways to give away your personal power.

Sean was in therapy for anger management because he lost his temper at work and hit a fellow coworker. Because he belonged to a union, instead of termination, the union intervened to give Sean a second chance.

Red in the face and punching a fist into the palm of his other hand, Sean explained the incident at work. He was still angry.

"He made me so angry. He really pissed me off. It's his fault that I decked him."

The pronoun "I" is a power word, a responsibility word.

I told Sean, "The pronoun, 'I' is a power word, a responsibility word. "'I chose to get angry' is a power state-ment, which allows you the option to choose a different behavior next time. Why are you giving away your personal power to this other person?"

It took a few sessions for Sean to realize he was responsible for his own emotions, but when he did, his anger control improved.

To the adolescents reading this book, if you have lazy or dysfunctional parents who don't care what you do as long as you don't disturb or inconvenience their lives, then you must be even more careful about your decisions and behaviors. You are walking the tightrope of adolescence without a safety net. Rules help to keep you safe.

> **Rules protect us from ourselves**

Positive Direction Intervention

1. What is one rule that you resist?
2. Will resisting that rule cause you problems in the future?
3. Be honest – is the rule causing the problem or is your attitude or response to the rule causing problems? You can't change the world, but you can change how you respond to the world.
4. Write down ways you can respond differently to rules that you resist following. What are the benefits of making this change?

Diva Pookie Boop

Solution 10: Accept - Learn - Avoid Repetition

Every human makes mistakes; this is how we learn. You often learn more from your mistakes because pain is a powerful teacher. However, you can also learn from another person's painful mistakes. It's not necessary to learn everything the hard way.

> **You are destined to repeat mistakes that you do not learn.**

You must be willing to accept your mistakes, or your part in a situation, to be able to benefit from the lesson.

I was visiting Lafayette, Louisiana, to celebrate the backcountry Mardi Gras. There were several cars of friends following Hal, because he was the only one who knew the way to a dance venue. Hal sped up and followed another car through a red light, leaving the rest of us lost. We all eventually found our way. After I parked, I confronted Hal about the traffic light he ran.

> **It is *not* necessary to learn everything the hard way.**

"I didn't run the red light," Hal. said

"I was right behind you. I saw you run the red light!"

"The guy in front of me ran the red light, I just followed him," Hal said.

"If he ran it and you followed him, then you ran it, too."

"No I didn't run the light, he did," Hal said.

Hal was likely to repeat this mistake and I would be interested to hear the police officer's reaction to his illogical explanation.

> **Reduce your pain level in life by not repeating your mistakes.**

You are destined to repeat mistakes that you don't acknowledge. Albert Einstein once said, "We cannot solve our problems with the same thinking we used when we created them." Twelve Step programs often teach, "Insanity is doing the same thing over and over again and expecting different results." Reduce your pain level in life by *not* repeating your mistakes. They are painful enough the first time, without dishing up a second helping.

If you are truly wise, you will avoid making mistakes that you see others make. Why suffer unnecessary pain? The life you are trying to create is one with less pain and more joy.

Positive Direction Intervention

Think of one mistake from your past. List all the lessons you could have learned from this mistake. Write them down. If you do this, you will transform that mistake from a liability to an asset.

Inspirational Thought

Diva Pookie Boop

Diva Pookie Boop

Solution 11: Every Time You Repeat a Mistake, the Consequences Get Worse

If you don't study for a test or turn in your homework, your grades will decline. That affects your college choices, which affects your career, which eventually affects how much money you earn, which affects your standard of living and retirement. Did you know that a bachelor's degree could increase your lifetime earnings by a half-million dollars?

This principle applies to everyone at every age. For example, if you don't pay bills in a timely manner, a late charge is levied, and it is reported on your credit rating. Every additional time that you pay late, you pay another late charge, and your credit rating suffers.

Who cares about a credit rating? You should, because it can affect your ability to rent the apartment you want someday, your ability to qualify for a loan for a house, or to get a loan to buy a car, among other things. When you continue to repeat mistakes, other people lose respect for you and they won't trust your opinion or judgment. Family and friends using good sense won't be willing to risk their good credit to cosign a loan with you.

> **If you are currently in a downward trend, turn it around by doing something different, a more positive behavior.**

Mike leaned forward, elbows on his knees, with his face in his hands as he told me his story.

"I don't know what I am going to do. I moved my family down here and the kids have finally settled into school, and now this happens."

Mike had problems with managing his money. As a result, he was in debt and felt helpless to get out. An attorney advised him to file for bankruptcy.

"I have a security clearance and a bankruptcy could affect my job. I saw a debt-reduction counselor several years ago, but I didn't have the discipline to follow his suggestions. Now I wish I had; I wouldn't be worried about losing my job."

> **Each baby step in the right direction leads to change.**

If you are currently in a downward trend, turn it around by doing something different, a more positive behavior. Start a budget, cut expenses, and take control of your finances. Each baby step in the right direction leads to change. It is never too late to change a bad habit and to improve your situation. Just do the next right thing. Small changes can help you create your deepest desires.

Positive Direction Intervention

1. What bad habit have you repeated? Write it down.

2. What has it cost you thus far? Write it down

3. What could it cost you in the future? Write it down. If you don't like this trend, do the right thing and change it.

Inspirational Thought

Diva Pookie Boop

Diva Pookie Boop

Solution 12: "The Platinum Rule"

You may have heard of the "Golden Rule."

"Do unto others as you would have them do unto you." Confucius

Confucius was a Chinese teacher and philosopher who lived from 551-479 BCE and who preceded Christ.

Jesus of Nazareth advocated the same principle. "Therefore all things whatsoever ye would that men should do to you, do ye even so to them: for this is the law and the prophets." Matthew 7:12

"And as ye would that men should do to you, do ye also to them likewise." Luke 6:31

Jesus Christ was the founder of the Christian Church. His disciples documented his life and teaching into the four gospels.

In recent history, a different variation of this principle is highlighted in the book, "Platinum Rule," written by Tony Alessandra and Michael O'Conner. "Treat other people the way *they* want to be treated." I suggest you read it.

> **"Treat other people the way they want to be**

Walt was in therapy because his marriage was in jeapordy. His wife felt he was insensative to her needs and desires. He decided to buy her a gift for her birthday and wanted my opinion.

"I'm thinking of buying Alice this great little lightweight rod I saw at the store," said Walt. He sat on the edge of his seat, clearly excited about the idea.

By the Golden Rule, Walter would buy Alice a fishing rod, because that is what he would want someone to purchase for him. Unless Alice loves to fish, she may not be pleased with this choice.

"Walt, does Alice like to fish?"

"Oh, she goes fishing with me every once in a while." Walt sat back in his seat.

"How often is that Walt?"

"Hmmm, maybe two or three times a year." His leg started bouncing.

"Does she already have a fishing rod?"

"Well yeah, she has two. What are you getting at here Doc?"

"Can you think of anything else Alice might like? Has she hinted about anything?"

He scrunched his face while he considered the question. "She's been going on and on about these earrings she saw at the mall."

"I suggest you buy her the earrings, Walt."

By the Platinum Rule, Walt would buy Alice a gift she would enjoy, like the earrings that he saw her admire at the mall. This may not seem like a practical gift to Walt, but the gift isn't for him.

Walt did buy Alice the earrings and he had a happy and grateful wife as a result.

In general, treat others with kindness, consideration, and respect. If the whole world operated by this rule, there would be much less strife and more happiness. Happiness is important.

Positive Direction Intervention

Apply the "Platinum Rule" by performing one small act of kindness today. Small actions can have a big impact.

Inspirational Thought

Diva Pookie Boop

Diva Pookie Boop

Solution 13: Garbage In = Garbage Out

Information or beliefs taught to you by your family may not be accurate. Sometimes misinformation is passed from generation to generation with the best of intentions. Much of it could be correct. However, dysfunctional families teach a higher percentage of faulty information than functional families.

Irene was definitely a victim of erroneous beliefs that her critical father had consistently programmed into her mind.

"I could never do anything good enough to please my dad. He never once told me that I did something good, he only pointed out what I did wrong." Irene rocked back and forth in the chair and clutched a throw pillow across her chest like a shield.

"His favorite thing to say to me was 'I can't believe you were so stupid.'"

In reality, Irene was a very intelligent lady. Due to faulty mental programming by her father, she believed she was stupid. In order for Irene to be happy, she would need to throw out the negative auditory programming planted in her mind by her father.

A big step for Irene was to realize that her dad was human and could make mistakes. I asked her to take an IQ test and she scored very high. It helped her to see in black and white that her dad made a mistake about her intelligence.

Your friends could also be sharing flawed data. How many times were you told gossip that wasn't true? Even the

Internet is a mixture of fact and fiction. The world is in a high tech information age and it's your task to determine what is true or false.

The human brain and a computer have many things in common. If incorrect information is put into the system, what comes out won't be accurate either; hence, Wilf Hey's saying, "Garbage in, garbage out."

Be careful about the data you allow to be stored on the personal hard drive, in your brain. You evaluate new information and experiences on a daily basis. Should you store that information in your brain and use it, or discard it?

One of the developmental tasks of adolescence is to construct your moral code. This is done by evaluating what you were taught, what you saw others do, what you read, and what you observed in media. Then make decisions about what is the right thing to do and the best way to live. Try to hold on to what is true, good, and healthy, and discard the rest.

This task continues into adulthood. Healthy adults constantly evaluate and revise their beliefs and moral code, by incorporating new information and experiences.

Examine your beliefs. Your beliefs set up the framework of how you look at life and the world. That looking glass becomes your perception, how you see the world and yourself. Your perception can affect your thinking.

> **You begin creating your life direction through your thoughts, words, and actions.**

Edit your thoughts carefully, because they precede your feelings and behaviors. You think before you act. Our brains are lightening fast and efficient, so we often don't realize that we think before we act.

To what music do you listen, what do you read, what games do you play, and what visual media do you watch? Is it positive and inspiring or negative and violent? What data are you downloading to your brain?

If you think watching violence in media doesn't affect you in a negative way, ask any police officer or active duty soldier, who has witnessed violence as part of their job. You carry those gruesome images in your brain forever and your mind tries to numb your reaction to help you cope.

If you *choose* to repeat the negative behavior patterns of your family and friends, these behaviors can develop into entrenched habits, which can set you up for recurrent life trauma, known as the Black Hole. You set patterns into the neural pathways of your brain on a daily basis. Make those pathways ones for positive, healthy behaviors and habits. Once those habits are entrenched and developed, you unconsciously repeat them. Do you think about your route to work or school, or do you drive there on automatic pilot, because it is an entrenched pattern on your personal hard drive? Negative habits are difficult to change, so it is best to avoid them.

> **Negative habits are difficult to change, so it is best to avoid them.**

If family members or friends are doing something that is ruining their lives, avoid doing the same, or you will suffer the same results. *Stop the Craziness* before it starts if possible. That thinking or behavior is garbage, so don't store it in your mind.

Think before you speak, for words are powerful and carry energy to promote wondrous good or tremendous harm. You begin creating your life direction through your thoughts, words, and actions.

Keep your thoughts pure, accurate, and positive. Keep the treasures, but regularly throw out the garbage, just as you would junk mail. Delete! Delete! Delete!

Positive Direction Intervention

1. What inaccurate beliefs are keeping you from the life you deserve? If you just thought, *I don't deserve a good life, because I'm a bad person,* that is a negative and faulty belief to work on immediately.
2. Write down as many inaccurate beliefs as you can identify and then go seek the truth from a reliable source.

Inspirational Thought

Diva Pookie Boop

Diva Pookie Boop

Solution 14: Life is Like a Garden

Life and gardens both have lots of manure. Manure in a garden can accumulate and stink, or you can mix it into the soil and use it as fertilizer to grow things. If you decide to stockpile your negative life events (emotional manure), you will stink up your life. Negative events can serve to season and mature you.

You will always have some negative events in your life; how you use them makes all the difference. My husband, Bob and I love to dance, especially ballroom dancing. Dancing improves our memories, our fitness level, our endurance, provides socialization, and improves our marital relationship. We dance three to four times a week. I saw a podiatrist after I injured my left foot, while running in heels to arrive on time for an event. After x-rays, the doctor told me I had either a stress fracture or a partial ligament tear. I would be on crutches a minimum of six weeks. (In reality, it was three months.) I held my emotions inside until I reached my car, where I could call Bob on my mobile phone.

> **Negative events serve to season and mature you.**

Sobbing, I told Bob, "I won't be able to dance for six weeks or longer!"

For a short space of time, I felt as if my world, as I knew it, had ended. Indeed, it had, but a new one was unfolding before my very eyes. I had a choice, manure or fertilizer. I chose fertilizer. I learned to adapt and live my life on crutches and an occasional spin in a wheelchair, grateful that the situation wasn't permenant. I even attended the Cotton Ball, a dance event, in a wheelchair. I made a trip to the beach. I found my crutches worked better on sand than walking. I even played miniature golf on crutches. I never missed a day of work. My office was on the second floor of a building with no elevator.

I gained many benefits from my injury. I learned that Bob and I enjoyed many things together, other than dancing. Bob was indeed there for me, in sickness and health. When I returned to dancing, I found I had improved my balance, through the necessity of standing on one leg. I rediscovered that I was a resourceful person. The most important thing I learned, was a smidgen of what life is like while living with a diasability.

My beautiful yard wouldn't exist today, if it weren't for my injury. The time I couldn't spend dancing, I utilized to research and draw the landscaping plan for my front and rear gardens. Every day we enjoy our own secret garden, which was the benefit of my injury.

> **Negativity can grow just as well as positive thoughts in your mind.**

Even if you make good choices and use your life manure as fertilizer, you still need to plant wisely. Weeds grow just as well as flowers in a garden. Negativity can grow just as well as positive thoughts in your mind. Just like a garden, a poorly maintained life will proliferate with weeds that choke out the good things. Negative thoughts and people can choke your garden with weeds.

Successful gardens also need water and sun. Water and sun are to a garden, what nurturing and love are to a human.

Do you feel like the weeds are encroaching on your life, choking out all your joy? Are you pulling those weeds out of your life—all those negative people and even your own negative thoughts about yourself and others? Are you seeking out the right people to love and nurture you? If not, start pulling weeds now and plant the seeds for a happier future.

Positive Direction Intervention

1. What are the weeds in your life? Write them down and start weeding your life!
    a. What are your negative thought weeds?
    b. What are your emotional garbage weeds?
    c. What are your destructive habit weeds?
    d. What are your inaccurate belief weeds?
2. Don't become discouraged if you have many weeds. Just pull one weed at a time. Often weeds are interconnected, so when you pull one out, several come out at the same time. That's less effort for you.

Diva Pookie Boop

Solution 15: Be Nice to Yourself

It is important to be your own best friend, that way your best friend can go with you everywhere. Nurture yourself, love yourself, stop the negative self-talk, and say nice things to yourself. There are many people willing to talk trash to bring others down, don't do it to yourself.

> **Be your own best friend.**

Accept yourself: Yes even all of your flaws. Are you placing your flaws under your own personal microscope, magnifying them to huge proportions? If so, stop it! Everyone has flaws; no person is perfect.

I was passing out the mid-term exam to my psychology class. Maureen ran from the classroom holding her hand over her mouth.

"Where is Maureen going," I asked.

Several students simultaneously responded, "To throw up."

"Does she always get sick before tests?"

"Every time," one of the students responded.

Maureen returned with downcast eyes, visibly shaking and she slid down in her seat. After class, I asked her if she was ill or experiencing test anxiety. Apparently, she had been wrestling with test anxiety since elementary school.

I met with Maureen before the next class and taught her some anxiety control techniques and test taking skills.

The major culprit of her test anxiety was her negative self-talk. She was telling herself negative statements such as:

1. "I know I will forget everything I studied."
2. "I know I am going to flunk this test."
3. "I am such a loser."
4. "I know I will get sick and look stupid in front of all these people."

Maureen was setting up a self-fulfilling prophesy by telling her unconscious mind her fears. The unconscious mind behaves as your own personal Genie. She thought it, so therefore; her unconscious mind created the reality. Maureen was verbally abusing herself in an unkind and cruel way.

Maureen started using multisensory deep breathing and positive self-talk such as:

1. "I know this material. This will be easy.
2. "I am going to get a good grade on this test."
3. "I am smart and a good student."
4. "I feel calm and at peace."

Maureen never again was sick before a test and her lower levels of anxiety helped to improve her test scores.

> **Never wallow in misery. Pig's wallow, humans overcome.**

Just as verbal self-abuse is unacceptable, so is physical self-abuse. Don't harm your body by starving it, scarring it with cuts, or damaging it with drugs and alcohol.

An ancient Roman philosopher, Publius Syrus coined the maxim "Misery loves company." However, when in misery, the best action is to do something helpful and healthy to leave misery behind. Never wallow in misery. Pig's wallow, humans overcome.

If you need help to deal with emotional pain, ask for help. If you need help with an addiction, seek treatment. There are people willing to help you. Just ask. Check the phone book or online for options.

There are enough people in this world to be mean to you without being mean to yourself. After all, this is a lifelong journey, and you are making it with yourself. Be a good travel companion and your own best friend. Negative self-talk just slows you to a standstill.

Positive Direction Intervention

1. Try multisensory deep breathing. Imagine a color that you would associate with anxiety or nervousness. (For me this is a muddy grey and brown.) Now imagine the color you would associate with peaceful serenity. (I usually choose a light blue.) *Color is very individual; it doesn't matter what color you choose as long as it has meaning to you.* This is not a test; it is an experience. With closed eyes, you are going to *inhale* a deep breath of your *calming color to a count of six.* Slowly and *fully exhale* your *nervous color to a count of nine.* Do this for five repetitions. Keep your breathing slow and deep. This not only calms you, but it oxygenates your brain for clearer thinking. This may make you feel dizzy if you are a shallow breather.

Diva Pookie Boop

Solution 16: Play by the Rules

There are rules everywhere—some overt (stated and written down like laws) and some covert (not openly declared, but you are expected to know them by some miraculous means). Wise people learn the rules of where they live, work, and go to school, to avoid negative consequences such as being kicked out of the house, fired from their job, or expelled from school. Anytime you thumb your nose at a rule, you are inviting authority to enforce that rule. It is like a fly buzzing around a dinner plate whose behavior says, "Come swat me!"

Most rules exist because some unwise person(s) did something stupid, offensive, or self-serving that caused harm in some way. Consequently, we all pay for the bad behavior of a few people who never learned how to play the game of real life.

> **Anytime you thumb your nose at a rule, you are inviting authority to enforce that rule.**

Jason sprawled across my couch and nonchalantly flipped my throw pillow on the floor, while he cast a sideways glance in my direction to gauge my response. I decided he had triggered enough negative at-tention today through rebellious behaviors. I chose to not empower him through acknowledgement, and instead granted his parents my full attention.

The family was in my therapy office because the principle of Jason's school placed him in detention yesterday. According to Jason, the detention was for wearing his cap in school. According to his parents, a teacher asked him twice to remove his cap and then sent Jason to the principal. He became argumentative and was disrespectful to the principal, which resulted in two days of detention.

Jason told his parents, "It is a stupid rule; there is nothing wrong with my cap."

Indeed, there was nothing offensive about Jason's cap, but students before him had worn offensive or sexually explicit caps to school. The school system didn't want to enter into an incident-by-incident debate over what was appropriate, so they adopted the policy of good manners established centuries ago: A gentleman removes his hat when he enters a building.

I encouraged Jason to suggest a committee, comprised of students and teachers to approve acceptable hats. He could hone his leadership skills by volunteering for the committee.

Do all rules make sense or are they right? No, but most are in place for legitimate reasons, generally for our protection. If a rule needs to be changed, use the appropriate methods to try to change it, because open rebellion is inviting authority to swat you like a fly. If you do choose to sacrifice yourself in open rebellion, at least choose a good cause. Unnecessary conflict results in unhappiness, which is contrary to your goal.

Positive Direction Intervention

1. Are you engaging in pointless behavior, which only results in a painful swat by those in charge?
2. What is the lesson and what can you do differently? Write it down.

Inspirational Thought

Diva Pookie Boop

Diva Pookie Boop

Solution 17: Respect Yourself

You set the rules of engagement for your social interactions with other people. You teach people how to treat you.

You do this by what you say and do. It becomes clear in how you speak about yourself. It becomes apparent by the way, you treat your body and your belongings.

My cousin, Billy, worked hard, saved his money, and bought a new car. He took excellent care of it. He didn't allow food or beverages in his car. His friends complied with his boundaries and it didn't affect their friendship in any negative way. Billy even declared his boundaries with my father, in a respectful way.

> **You teach people how to treat you.**

"Uncle Charlie, I don't allow smoking in my car, would you please wait until we get back home."

"Sure Billy, I'm sorry I didn't even think about it. I know you don't smoke," said my Dad. "Where's your ashtray and I'll put it out?"

"My ash tray is clean Uncle Charlie, I'll pull over so you can put it out."

I was sitting in the back seat when this occurred. Later, I heard my Dad bragging on Billy because he stood up for what was important to him.

The same principle applies to your body and how you dress. While attending a hockey game with some friends, a lovely young teen with long blonde hair and too much makeup walked in front of us. She was wearing tight jeans and a revealing top. She was about fifteen, masquerading as a twenty-year-old. After she passed, the guy sitting next to me poked his friend in the ribs, pointed at the young lady and announced for all to hear, "She is definitely advertising! She's a billboard that says, 'Come get me. I will let you do anything you want.'" There were more unkind, sexually explicit comments, that I won't repeat.

We say a great deal about ourselves by what we wear. It may not be what we think it says. The young lady thought she was attractive. The men saw her as an easy mark. I wondered why her parents let her appear in public dressed in a manner that encouraged men to think of their daughter in such a depraved sexual way.

Remember, people only show you as much respect as you show yourself.

Positive Direction Intervention

Imagine yourself as a five-year-old. That precious child resides in you permanently. Understand that whatever you do to yourself; you do the same to that vulnerable little kid inside of you. He or she is depending on you, as the adult, to protect him or her. If you wouldn't allow a five-year-old to eat or drink something, be around certain people, or do certain things, then it would be a good idea for you to not do it either. That adorable internal child travels with you everywhere.

Inspirational Thought

Diva Pookie Boop

Diva Pookie Boop

Solution 18: Respect Others

You set the rules of engagement for your social interactions. When you treat others with kindness and respect, it sets the tone for the whole interaction. Sometimes it can even change the interaction.

While attending college, I worked as a clerk at a drug store. When I encountered a rude, whiny, or otherwise unpleasant customer, I refused to respond in kind. I was unwilling to let a negative customer ruin my good mood. Instead, I cheerfully smiled and treated Mr. Grumpy Pants or Ms. Panties-in-a-Wad in a respectful, pleasant, and courteous manner. On nearly every occasion, the customer changed his or her demeanor to become more pleasant. It is difficult to be unkind, when people are courteous to you, without appearing foolish. On each occasion that I changed a sourpuss into a smiling customer, I felt as if I had won a minor victory for the world. I sent a more pleasant person into society, instead of unleashing an even angrier person to do more harm. I'm not saying this was always easy.

> **When you treat others with kindness and respect, it sets the tone for the whole interaction. Sometimes it can even change the interaction.**

I found the same to be true while working in an alcohol and drug Intensive Outpatient Program (IOP). Many of my first encounters with patients started on a negative note. They were snarly, angry, defensive, and rude. These patients were angry about coming to the assessment, felt forced to be there, and had convinced themselves that they didn't have a problem. I understood that they weren't angry with me, but was angry with themselves and the situation. Somewhere deep inside each of those patients, they knew that their behavior set up the conditions that resulted in their consequences, but wasn't ready to admit it yet.

I often heard, "I don't have a problem, I am being forced to be here."

I would reply, "You don't have to enter this program. I can contact your court referral officer and tell him you would prefer to serve your time in jail and miss time from your job, rather than take this opportunity to improve yourself."

I would remain calm, pleasant, respectful and professional. Again, this wasn't always easy. It would be easier to be rude, but then I would be the one behaving badly. Two wrongs doesn't make a right. Most of the time, the other person's negative attitude would go away after ten minutes. Sometimes it would take nearly an hour. I can only think of three people in eight years of working in that position, that didn't eventually apologize to me for their initial negative behavior.

You have the power to influence the world by the way you show respect to others.

Positive Direction Intervention

See how many people you can influence in a positive way through an upbeat and respectful approach. You do make a difference.

Inspirational Thought

Let your light shine. Set a positive path for others to follow. Look for the shining goodness in others.

Diva Pookie Boop

Diva Pookie Boop

Solution 19: Life is a Process

Life is about the process and the events of day-to-day living, not just the outcome. Each day exists to cherish and enjoy. Live each moment fully in order to construct a fulfilling life.

I often hike with my husband. We walk along the trail, enjoy the scent of the trees, admire the scenery, and feel refreshed by the breeze. We enjoy each other's company, while sharing meaningful conversation. We share little discoveries we make along the path. The whole experience of walking the trail and being with someone I love is what is important, not advancing to the end of the trail. Each day is a fresh start, a chance to change your life into something better.

> **Live each moment fully in order to construct a fulfilling life.**

No, you can't change your past, but you don't live in the past. *You live in today.* Make each day count by doing some small act of kindness, uplift another person, or do something to help the environment. It doesn't have to be anything large, because one small kind act may be passed from person to person to improve the world. Tiny steps change behaviors, correct problems, or help to attain a goal.

Unfortunately, one wrong decision or careless action can create a crisis in your life. Those disasters take time to resolve. Each small step you take to resolve a problem or to improve your situation adds up to big pay-offs.

> **Each day is a fresh start, a chance to change your life into something better.**

Samantha accepted a new position and moved to another city after completing college. In her excitement, she signed a lease for an apartment that was barely within her budget and proceeded to furnish it with what she truly loved. Unfortunately, this started her new life with credit card debt.

When Samantha returned home to visit, she came to see me, because she didn't want to admit her problem to her parents.

"I love my apartment, but I don't have any money left to enjoy my life. I'm apartment poor. I can't save money. I worry about my bills all the time."

Fortunately for her, the credit debt was five thousand and not twenty thousand dollars or more. We discussed how this financial crisis occurred.

"I guess I grew up having everything I wanted immediately, but mom and dad weren't paying for it this time."

> **Small actions can make a huge difference.**

Like so many people in our society, Samantha fell prey to immediate gratification. We discussed several options and Samantha chose a wise path that was not quick and easy, but better for her in the end. She chose to tutor some children in her apartment complex in math and applied all the proceeds to clear her credit card debt. She managed to do this in less than a year. The process of having to correct her own mistake, instead of allowing her parents pay off her debt, imbedded in her mind the importance of a budget and thinking before she spends in the future. In addition, she helped several of her students improve their grades and met many of her neighbors. This helped her to adjust to her new living environment. Small actions can make a huge difference.

> **Don't sit down and live your life in your memories. Get up and create new ones.**

If you are older, don't think it is too late to make a difference. This just means you have less time to get started. Don't sit down and live your life in your memories. Get up and create new ones.

> **Make death chase you while you experience that one last swallow of life.**

Make a positive impact on the people you love and the world around you. Don't sit down and wait for the end.

If you are a teen, enjoy your youth and this wonderful time of lesser responsibilities and fun events. This will only happen during this time of your life. Don't rush to grow up too fast and move to the end of your journey, which is death.

> **Wake up; shake off your stupor, open your eyes, and see everything.**

Dodge the mundane. Avoid stumbling through your life in a trance, barely aware of the beauty all around you. Wake up; shake off your stupor, open your eyes, and see everything. Make every moment count. Be acutely aware of all that surrounds you, so you don't miss anything. Make death chase you while you experience that one last swallow of life.

Positive Direction Intervention

For one hour, be like Sherlock Holmes, the famous fictional detective who had extraordinary powers of observation. See, smell, feel, and hear everything around you. Be aware of all the things that you normally tune out. You will be amazed at what you have missed that was there, waiting to be discovered. Stop sleepwalking through your life. Life is a process. Don't miss one minute of joy from that process. Life is not car race around a track. Life is a wonderful journey down a winding road. Slow down, so you don't speed past it.

Inspirational Thought

Beauty can be appreciated by the contrasts in our lives. We appreciate warmth after being cold. We enjoy the light of day after the dark of night. Sad times help us to treasure the happy times.

Diva Pookie Boop

Diva Pookie Boop

Solution 20: Your Time Is Priceless

You can reach into your pocket and spend money, confident that you will have the opportunity to earn more. Imagine if the money you had in your pocket must last the rest of your life, and once it was gone, you would perish. Would you spend it wisely?

When you were born, LIFE opened your "time bank account." The amount of time deposited will remain a mystery. It could be seconds or decades. Time is your most precious possession. When you reach into your life and commit your time—it is gone *forever*. You can't earn more time.

Do you cherish your time with the people you love or are you taking them for granted? Have the people in your life become like furniture, something that you walk past while you live your life?

> **Time is your most precious possession. When you reach into your life and commit your time—it is gone *forever*. You can't earn more time.**

I remember the day I received the call that my dad was having a heart attack. I raced to the hospital in a panic. I was afraid he might die before I saw him. What consoled me as I sped my way through traffic was that I told him, "I love you Dad", and hugged him on our last lunch together. Actually, I couldn't tell you how many times I expressed my love for my father, because it was a habit for me. I never missed an opportunity to show or tell him. Have you hugged the people important to you today?

I arrived in time. My dad survived a triple bypass operation on his heart. He lived and had many productive years. When my father died from cancer many years later, I was by his side, telling him I loved him and holding his hand.

> **With life, you don't know your expiration date.**

Your time is irreplaceable—are you wasting it with negative people and activities? Are you squandering your precious time on meaningless activities, such as computer games and television? At least with money, you can count it and know how much you have left. With life, you don't know your expiration date.

Yes, you have an expiration date. Do you have one week or eighty years? Spend your time wisely. Cherish each moment as if it might be your last. Youth isn't a guarantee of tomorrow, because young people die every day.

Positive Direction Intervention

Have you told the important people in your life how much you care? It's never too late to start. Do it immediately. Tomorrow may be too late. Write down the names of the people you will contact.

Inspirational Thought

Be careful that your point of view doesn't keep you from seeing the whole situation. Blocking out information could lead to poor decisions. Take off your blinders.

Diva Pookie Boop

Stop the Craziness: Simple Life Solutions

Diva Pookie Boop

Solution 21: Listen

People love to talk, but seldom do people listen. How many times have you tuned out after a few words or sentences? Have you ever missed the point of a discussion, because you started to formulate your response or counterattack? If you are astute, you will become a good listener. If you are a good listener, you will learn much about motivation, driving forces, and human nature.

If you listen attentively to others, you will attract many friends who will consider you a sage and a valuable friend. Listen to what people say, but also tune in for missing information. Most importantly, listen to what people communicate through their actions and behaviors. If the behavior doesn't match a person's stated intentions, believe the behavior. The limbic brain will communicate through the body (actions), before the frontal cortex (thinking), has time to form a verbal response.

> **If you are a good listener, you will learn much about motivation, driving forces, and human nature.**

Marge and Bill were having marital problems. They sat on opposite sides of my office sofa, and piled the decorative pillows between them. Marge had listed a number of suspicious behaviors, which led her to believe her husband was involved in an extramarital affair. After telling me her list of evidence, she looked at her husband of seven years in the eye and asked, "Bill are you having an affair with another woman?"

Bill looked her steadily in the eye, began bouncing his right leg, and moved his head in an affirmative up and down movement, and answered, "No, I'm not having an affair."

> **Believe action any day over the flapping of someone's lips.**

I didn't believe him and neither did Marge. Over the next couple of weeks, Marge scoured Bill's cell phone records and guessed the password to his email. He had been having an affair for at least three months. Bill admitted the truth only when confronted with the hard evidence. Believe action any day over the flapping of someone's lips.

By listening carefully to others, you will gain the power of information, and it is one key to success in life. Develop radar ears and use what you learn wisely. If you would like to learn more about listening to body language with your eyes read, "What Every Body is Saying", by Joe Navarro with Marvin Karlins, Ph.D.

Positive Direction Intervention

1. Listen with your ears and your eyes.
2. Focus on what people are saying to you, as if you had to repeat back what they just told you. Ask questions if there is any confusion. Try it with your best friend.
3. Watch body language and facial expressions that reveal comfort or discomfort. Look for the base rate of common body gestures, so you can tell when there is a different behavior. As Joe Navarro cautions, changes in body language reveal changes in thoughts or emotions. This gives you an opportunity to ask more questions that explains the "why".

He cautions you not to assume you know the reason for the change in behavior. These behaviors are known as "tells". Just don't assume you know what the behavior is telling you, without further investigation.

Stop the Craziness: Simple Life Solutions 109

Diva Pookie Boop

Solution 22: Just Because Your Friends Do It...

My mother had a saying that she learned from her mother, who probably learned it from generations before her.

"Just because your friends jumped off a bridge, does it mean you should jump off one, too?"

I heard it so often, that when my mother started the sentence, I would typically finish it for her. Humans like to follow trends, so if everyone is doing something, it seems the right thing to do. This is not necessarily true. During World War II, Hitler sent thousands of Jews to the gas chambers. Many people were involved in the executions, but it didn't make it right. History is full of trends that caused great harm. Two good questions to ask yourself: Is this right for me? Does it cause harm?

> **Two good questions to ask yourself: Is this right for me? Does it cause harm?**

We are all different. Dancing is the most pleasurable exercise for me. It may be torture for you. I love it because it is fun, aerobic, keeps my mind sharp, and is a form of socialization. You may be able to run with no ill effect, but your friend may find that running injures his knees. The latest fashion craze may look great on a runway model but not on you. Should you wear it anyway and look horrible?

I recently enjoyed a beautiful day with my husband at the park. A large and attractive lady was feeding the ducks with her daughter and grandchild. She was dressed in a trendy fashion similar to her slender daughter, who appeared to be in her twenties.

The jeans and top were stylish and attractive. However, on her, they only emphasized her figure flaws and caused her to "muffin top" over the waistline of the jeans. Her clothing was clearly not comfortable. Every time she bent over to assist her grandchild, her jeans slid down her backside revealing parts of her anatomy best not exposed in public. She had to grab her jeans and yank them up repeatedly. She was clearly dressed to be in style, not in what was most attractive and comfortable for her.

> **Be an original, instead of a copy.**

A short time later, I observed a teenager doing his best to look cool, but failing miserably. He wore a matching tank top and knee-length shorts. While the outfit was stylish, the shorts were so large that he had to hold the front with his left hand, while walking with his legs in a wide stance to keep them from falling off. They hung halfway down his backside revealing his boxer shorts. This wide-legged stance resulted in a straight-legged waddle, which mimicked the ducks waddling behind him. There is nothing cool or masculine about waddling like a duck. He had his cell phone held to his ear with his right hand and his shorts clutched in his left. If anyone attacked him, he would be defenseless; he would have to drop his phone, his pants, or both to defend himself.

Be an original, instead of a copy. Remember, just because your friends do something, this doesn't mean it is the best path for you. This is true in business, too. Some of the most inventive people in our society chose a different, more original path. Do you want to copy a trend or be a trend?

Consider what negative things *could* happen and make wise choices, because you will live with the consequences, possibly for the rest of your life.

> **Do you want to copy a trend or be a trend?**

I knew a man who after partying with friends, attempted to drive home while under the influence of alcohol. All his friends left and drove home, so he thought he could too. He had a car accident. He killed a young woman and her infant. He served an eight-year sentence for Driving Under the Influence (DUI) and vehicular homicide.

He will eventually get out of jail, but he can't bring those people back to life. He is imprisoned with the memories of what he did forever.

Positive Direction Intervention

What is one behavior you are doing that is not the best choice for you. Consequences can last a lifetime. Be courageous. Change it.

Diva Pookie Boop

Solution 23: Write Down Your Goals

In order to get what you want in life, you must first know what you desire. I know this sounds simple. Millions of people are unsuccessful because they don't know exactly what they want in life. Your goals need to be clear and concise, instead of vague.

Would you go to the drive-in window of your favorite restaurant and say, "I'm not sure what I want, just give me something"? No, you wouldn't. So, why approach your future in this manner? Do some research about what you enjoy and what makes you happy. What are your talents and what are careers in those areas? How much education or training is required and how well does it pay? Your school guidance counselor at your high school or local college can help you with some of this information. I have referred many adults seeking a second career to local colleges to gain information. Information is power—if you use it.

> **Your goals need to be clear and concise, instead of vague.**

Don't choose a career in which you are not interested, no matter how much pressure you receive. If you choose the wrong career you will be unhappy, frustrated, and probably not excel. Your lack of motivation or abilities will inhibit your success. However, keep economics in mind, since you will live on the money generated by that career. You are the one who has to work eight-plus hours a day in your career until you retire.

So how do you write a goal? Here are some examples of what works and what doesn't.

1. A poorly written goal:
    a. "I *may* want to go to college."
    b. "I *want* a better job."
    c. An average written goal: "I *am* going to college."
    d. "I *am* going to look for a better job."
    e. A well written goal: "I *will* start The University of Alabama in the fall and I *will* graduate with an electrical engineering degree in four years."
    f. "I *will* apply for the project manager position in my office with an updated resume by Friday."

If, as an adult, you feel you made the wrong choice in a career, know it's never too late to have a successful second career. People do it all the time.

This book is a product of a third career for me. I wanted to share what I teach people in my therapy office, but on a broader scale. I had no idea how to get a book published, but I did know what I wanted to share with you and I knew how to program my mind to make it happen. This book began with a dream, some information, and a written goal. You can accomplish your goals if I can accomplish mine.

Visualize your goal as if it is happening.

Visualize your goal as if it is happening. When your unconscious has a clear message of where to steer you, it will. If it doesn't have clear instructions, you will drift off course.

So why put so much focus on our unconscious mind? A large part of our behavior each day is unconscious. We operate on autopilot while driving to work, getting ready in the morning, and doing other daily tasks. Why not have our autopilot move us toward becoming our best selves.

Let's look at another example. Karen expressed frustration during one session, because she couldn't lose the twenty pounds she needed to lose. What she had been telling herself was "I *need* to lose twenty pounds." She found she would get close to her goal and shoot back up to her original weight.

I told her, "Your goal is stated incorrectly. You are saying you need to lose twenty pounds. Your unconscious won't put you in danger by letting your weight get too low. It has to keep adding the weight back on, so you can lose twenty pounds.

We rewrote her goal to read, "I am 120 pounds and I wear a perfect size 6." This worked and she stopped the yo-yo effect.

Positive Direction Intervention

Write down at least one precise goal you want to achieve. It doesn't have to be a huge goal. It can be a small one. Small goals pave the way for larger goals.

Diva Pookie Boop

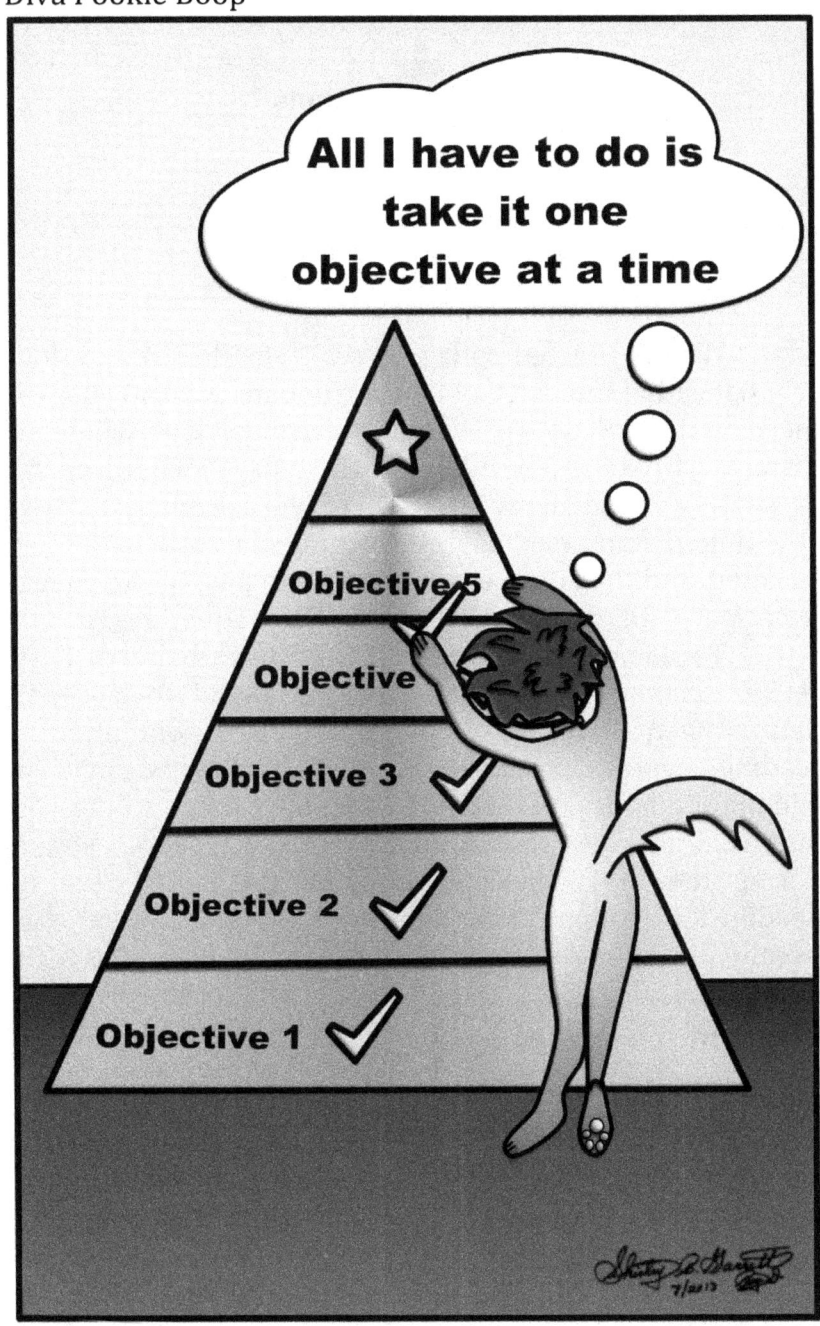

Solution 24: Break Goals into Small Parts Called Objectives

When I started college, I realized I had a long four years ahead of me before I could graduate. If I had counted the days (1,079 days), I would have been overwhelmed. Instead, I broke it down into small steps. I focused on the present. I applied all my attention to one assignment or test at a time. I immersed myself into my classes, classmates, learning, and the social events that were part of the college experience. All too soon, it was time for graduation.

To avoid the feeling of being overwhelmed, I use certain techniques to break a goal or task into workable parts. When I was in graduate school, I committed to reading several chapters in my textbooks every day. This eliminated hours of extended reading time at the last minute. I also researched and wrote my research papers during the first weeks of class, when there were no deadlines looming. Later when the papers were due, usually during mid-term or final exams, I only had to focus on studying for my tests.

It is much easier to see solutions on paper than to try to organize problems in your head.

Later, when I worked at a mental health center, the records librarian would unload a stack of twenty-five or more charts onto my desk every month and announce, "Here are all the charts you need to close this month, have fun!"

"Why are there so many? Are you giving me the entire center's charts to close?"

I'd look at that tall pile and think: *I'm never going to finish all of those.* Then I realized it wasn't a hard task. I just felt intimidated by the sheer number of charts. I put the pile of charts in a file drawer, so I wouldn't see them. I placed one chart on my desk. That looked easier, so I quickly finished that chart and put it in a different file drawer. Then I repeated the process and quickly finished the project with ease.

Another tip is to organize things on paper when you feel overwhelmed. It is much easier to see solutions on paper than to try to organize problems in your head.

It also reduces the amount of mental energy you expend. So, write it down. Make a to-do list. Put items on your computer, phone, or calendar that you wish to do and set reminders to assist your memory.

When making decisions, do a pros and cons list. Rate each pro and con with a number system. 1 = low importance. 2 = moderate importance. 3 = high importance. After rating the pros and cons, add up the scores. The results may show a clearer path.

Use the tools around you and take small steps each day toward your goals.

Positive Direction Intervention26

1. Take your goal and write down all the baby steps it will take to accomplish it.
2. On another piece of paper, write the steps down in the correct order. These are your objectives.
3. Work on them, one at a time, every day. Small steps lead to huge progress.

Inspirational Thought

Diva Pookie Boop

Stop the Craziness: Simple Life Solutions

Diva Pookie Boop

Solution 25: Understand Your Genetics

We are our genes. Every cell in our body has a nucleus containing a string of our DNA. If you look at your genetic history now, and make adjustments in your lifestyle, you may prevent some pain and suffering later.

I personally hate pain and suffering, and avoid it if possible. I would like to encourage you to avoid it too. Pain and suffering make living a happy life more diffficult.

Both my mother and grandmother developed weight problems. The three contributing factors for them were genetics, poor eating habits, and lack of exercise. My doctor advised me that if I exercise on a regular basis and ate healthy, that I had a better chance of maintaining a healthy weight. This could reduce the risk or delay certain genetic health problems. I am now middle-aged, and by following good advice from my physician, I work daily to maintain good health.

> **If you look at your genetic history now, and make adjustments in your lifestyle, you may prevent some pain and suffering later.**

Did you know that a predisposition toward the destructive disease of addiction is genetic for some people? If you have family members with alcohol or drug issues, be careful and don't experiment with alcohol or drugs. You may be predisposed to become addicted more quickly and deeply than other people. I never treated an alcoholic or addict who believed they would become addicted. They all thought they would just hang out with their friends, do a little recreational use for fun, and would stop the alcohol and drugs at will. Their genes kicked in every time and then destroyed their health. If you're genetically predisposed, once addicted, you're always addicted.

Why is this important to you? You are trying to create a life of happiness. Sickness and addictions will rob you of your happiness.

Positive Direction Intervention

1. Talk to the people in your family about past generations.
2. Write down your family tree and note the physical problems, causes of death, and any addiction issues in your family. Seeing the results on paper may make it easier to determine what genetic problems run in your family. It may also help you to determine a prevention strategy.

Inspirational Thought

Diva Pookie Boop

Diva Pookie Boop

Solution 26: "It Is Easier to Avoid Temptation than to Resist It."

This was the sage advice given to me by my grandmother. It's harder to resist drugs if your friends are passing them around and they are encouraging you to try them.

I once had a patient whose probation officer caught him in a random drug-screen. He tested po-sitive for cocaine.

> **One moment in time can change the entire direction of your life.**

"I knew I might have to take a drug test on Monday, but I was hanging out with some of my friends. When they passed that crack pipe around, I didn't even think about what I was doing," he said.

> **If you avoid situations where you will encounter temptation, you will be less likely to do the wrong thing.**

"Hanging around your old playgrounds with old playmates may land you back in jail, " I said.

"I know, I am praying the judge is in a good mood."

It's difficult to resist cupcakes while standing in a bakery with the smell wafting around you. It's tempting to drink just to fit in at a party where others are drinking.

Therefore, as much as I hate to admit it, my grandmother was right. The truth is, she was right most of the time. If you avoid people and situations where you will encounter temptation, you will be less likely to do the wrong thing.

> **Temptation is patient, lurking along the edges of your mind, waiting for the opportunity to pounce.**

Tiffany was sixteen and knew addiction ran on both sides of her family. In fact, we had discussed it in a family session. I advised her it would be wise to avoid addictive substances, if pos-sible. With a "just this once" thought, she drank at a party. She quickly became in-toxicated, which affected her judgment. She had sex with a guy at the party and became pregnant. Now she is struggling to raise a child and complete college, while making ends meet with a part-time job. She is living at home and must delay her dream to have her own place. Later she told me, "I never realized that one night could change the rest of my life."

Often people think they are stronger than temptation, because they have resisted the lure before. Temptation is patient, lurking along the edges of your mind, waiting for the opportunity to pounce. We are all human and every man, woman, and child has weak moments. Why take the chance?

Positive Direction Intervention

1. Identify one area of life in which you are flirting with the lure of temptation.
2. How can you avoid it and prevent yourself from taking the bait? Write it down.

Inspirational Thought

Beauty exists whether we stop to appreciate it or not.
Take the time to enjoy the beauty around you everyday.

Diva Pookie Boop

Diva Pookie Boop

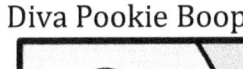

Solution 27: Avoid the Attitude of Entitlement

"The world doesn't owe you anything." This was a message I heard from my parents growing up and it is the truth. Believing in entitlement only weakens you. It makes you dependent on others and gives them power over you. It slows you down and keeps you from reaching your goals. I now realize my parents were trying to prepare me for the harsh reality of the world.

Parents are required by law to meet minimal standards in the care of their children: nutritious food, adequate shelter, basic clothing for the climate and season, medical care, and safety. They are required to do so until the child reaches the age determined by law as adulthood.

> **Believing in entitlement only weakens you. It makes you dependent on others and gives them power over you. It slows you down and keeps you from reaching your goals**

Anything you receive past those minimal standards, you should see as an additional benefit or a privilege. Adults and teens alike, have become confused about needs and desires. The following are *extra benefits*, which you may take for granted, which parents *aren't required* to provide:

1. Dinner out;
2. The soda or snacks of *your* choice;

3. The cost and transportation for you to play sports; take dance lessons, or music lessons;
4. The *latest fashion trends* in clothes or shoes;
5. A TV in your room;
6. A gaming system;
7. Skates;
8. A car (Many teens work to pay for at least part of the cost.);
9. A mobile phone (We existed without them for generations);
10. Spending money (Many teens earn their own);
11. A college education. (Many parents can't afford this.)

Those are all expensive and time-consuming *extras* for which parents generally have to work hard to acquire. They offer these *extras* out of love. Your parents don't have to provide these and shouldn't provide them forever. Isn't it nice when they do?

Part of the process of maturing is to work and earn these extravagances for yourself, so you can become independent. Adults and teens take a moment and think about all the luxuries your parents have provided for you over the years. Have you adequately expressed your gratitude to them?

Adults, are you setting your children up with an attitude of entitlement? Will they be able to take care of themselves when you're not there?

Positive Direction Intervention

Think about the opportunities and nice things others have provided for you. Thank them through your words and actions.

Inspirational Thought

Life is like water - it smoothes our rough edges and polishes us until we shine.

Diva Pookie Boop

Diva Pookie Boop

Solution 28: Attitude of Gratitude

My Dad was the sole income earner in my family. When I was seventeen, I watched my dad as he prepared his lunch to go to work. He worked the three-to-eleven shift as a remote-control train operator. He worked outdoors. This particular afternoon it was pouring rain, with temperatures hovering in the mid-thirties, with gusting winds. I arrived home from school, after walking the five blocks from the bus stop. I was ready to voice my complaints about how miserable I was from my ten-minute trek home. My dad greeted me with a smile and hug as I came into the kitchen. He was so pleased to see me and happily asked me questions about my day at school. He made no complaints about the weather, in which he was preparing to work in for the next eight hours. He worked because he loved us and was a responsible man.

> **Notice when people sacrifice for you and say thanks.**

I didn't complain about being cold or wet, because I knew my dad was about to endure much worse weather conditions for a longer period. Until that moment, I had never thought about the sacrifices my dad made for his family, because to be truthful, I was self-centered at that point in my life.

I hugged my Dad and told him, "Dad I love you and I really appreciate everything you do to support us. I know your job is hard…..umm… thanks."

Shocked, he hugged me and said, "Well, thank you Daughter Lou, I appreciate that you noticed. What do you want?"

"Nothing."

"Really, are you sure?"

"Yep, I just wanted to say thanks."

My dad was really in shock, because in the past, those spontaneous compliments usually led to a request for something.

I made a baby step toward maturity by thinking of someone other than myself. After that day, I made an effort to notice things that people did for me and was more demonstrative in my gratitude. Notice when people sacrifice for you and say thanks. You would want someone to notice your efforts and be appreciative, so do the same.

Positive Direction Intervention

For one day, notice every small thing that others do for you. You may be surprised.

Inspirational Thought

Diva Pookie Boop

Diva Pookie Boop

Solution 29: Guard Your Attitude

Another precious possession you should guard with your life is your attitude. Your attitude is the precursor to happiness or a miserable existence.

It also determines whether you will be a success or a failure at the tasks and goals that you undertake. Think of your attitude as the steering wheel of your life. Make sure you steer it in the right direction.

> **Your attitude is the precursor to happiness or a miserable existence.**

On the positive side, your attitude is part of you and comes from inside of you, not from others. Negative events and people can't control your attitude, unless you give them the power to do so. Therefore, your attitude is yours to control, positive or negative. It is your responsibility to guard your attitude from ne-gativity. A negative attitude can be contagious, like a cold or the flu. Through your conversations and actions, negativity can spread to your friends, coworkers and family. It can take days or weeks to recover.

> **A negative attitude can be contagious, like a cold or the flu. It can take days or weeks to recover.**

> **Negativity is mental poison**

Living in the negativity of others can make it even harder to overcome, because it wears you down. It can cause you to see negativity as normal, not dysfunctional. You can allow many things to shift your attitude in a positive or negative way, such as television, games, music, movies, books, and people. These choices are in your control. If you wouldn't swallow arsenic and poison your body, why would you fill your mind with negative people or media? Negativity is mental poison.

Positive Direction Intervention

1. Evaluate your environment for negativity. How many negative people, events, or media do you allow to infect your mind every week?
2. Do you think it would be in your best interest to make a positive change?

Inspirational Thought

Diva Pookie Boop

Diva Pookie Boop

Solution 30: Avoid Gossip

Gossip kills! It kills reputations, projects, marriages, relationships, businesses, and sometimes people. A school system, office, or manufacturing plant are the perfect environments to seed and grow gossip.

There is a communication principle that states: the more times a person hears specific information, the more likely that person is to believe it.

In other words, if everyone in school or the office is saying it, people will believe it must be true. Think about this false assumption. Suppose one person maliciously spreads false information to three people, and each of those three people come tell you what they heard. Are you likely to believe it was true? That is possible, since you heard it from three different people. Nonetheless, it was false information.

> **When you start or spread a rumor, you have no control over the outcome.**

I watched this happen to an acquaintance in high school. Someone started a rumor that Christine was pregnant. She was still a virgin, so this really upset her. As time progressed, she showed no signs of pregnancy. Instead of proving the rumor wrong, another rumor started that she'd had an abortion. Anyone who knew Christine knew she was opposed to abortion. There was no way to prove her innocence. This rumor caused her great mental anguish and damaged her reputation.

When you start or spread a rumor, you have no control over the outcome. Even if you know for absolute certainty a rumor is true, is it really anyone else's business?

Positive Direction Intervention

The next time you are tempted to pass on information that is no one's business, don't do it. You wouldn't want someone to do it to you. Think before you open your mouth.

Inspirational Thought

Diva Pookie Boop

Diva Pookie Boop

Solution 31: Don't Taunt or Be Unkind to Others

Small-minded people try to feel more successful by putting other people down. It's easy to be mean to the person who isn't as intelligent, attractive, socially connected, or a bit different in some way. People join their friends in this form of verbal and emotional abuse as a way to fit in with the crowd. Unfortunately, it has become a way of life for many people. It's called being a *bully*.

I once led a support group at a high school, which discussed common problems for teens. When I arrived for group one day, everyone was distraught. A student had committed suicide and had written in his suicide note that a contributing factor to his decision to end his life was the continuous verbal and emotional abuse that he'd endured at school every day. This student was dyslexic and struggled in school. Two of the boys in my group admitted that they had emotionally terrorized this student, and at the time, thought it was funny. They didn't realize the damage they inflicted on their fellow student. Others in the group had watched these two boys and others pick on that student and felt guilty for not stopping them.

> **It doesn't matter how you rationalize it, the verbal, emotional, or physical torture of a fellow human is not funny, professional, nor cool.**

After his death, these students felt personally responsible for the young man's suicide. No one is responsible for another person's choices or actions. However, these students were responsible for their cruel behavior, which contributed to that student's emotional instability.

This cruel form of emotional abuse is not limited to the classroom. I have had many patients seek counseling to cope with the stress of dealing with an office bully and cohorts. The snide comments, passive aggressive behaviors, and the sabotage that occurs in the workplace, rival that of any classroom. I once received a phone call from a capable professional woman who in tears wailed, "Dr. Garrett, make them stop talking about me." This highly competent person was reduced to child-like tears by the verbal and emotional cruelty of her co-workers.

It's sad to see children and adults behave in such hurtful ways. It doesn't matter how you rationalize it, the verbal, emotional, or physical torture of a fellow human is not funny, professional, nor cool.

Even more disturbing are the rash of shootings that have occurred nationwide in schools and businesses, often the product of bullying. Remember the Golden Rule, and change your behavior now.

Positive Direction Intervention

Refuse to initiate or participate in any form of abusive behavior of another person. If you can safely stop it, do so. If you can't safely stop it, call for help or report it.

Inspirational Thought

Diva Pookie Boop

Diva Pookie Boop

Solution 32: Find Something Positive in Every Situation

It is difficult to believe, but most situations have something positive. The positive outcome of a bad situation may be a lesson you learned, a skill you acquired, or simply a confirmation of your ability to endure.

> **The positive outcome of a bad situation may be a lesson you learned, a skill you acquired, or simply a confirmation of your ability to endure.**

I will always think of my dad as Mr. Silver Lining. One day he and I were running errands to prepare to leave for a trip the next day. We left a store and found we had a flat tire. My dad didn't curse, rant or throw things.

Rather than becoming upset, my dad looked at me and said, "We have a flat tire. This is a good opportunity for me to show you how to change a tire."

He calmly showed me what to do, step-by-step. Then as we were driving to the tire store to have the flat repaired, Dad said, "Aren't we lucky this happened today, while we are near the tire store and not tomorrow, when we would be on the open road?"

It's your choice; you can see bad things in good events or see good things in everything that happens. There are many things you can do to reduce the chance of bad things happening, but unfortunate circumstances happen to all of us. Look for something positive in every difficult situation. If it is difficult for you to discover anything good, find a "Silver Lining" friend to help you.

Reality is, that many times things don't go as planned. That is why back-up plans are so important for your peace of mind.

Positive Direction Intervention

1. Think about a challenging event in your life that recently occurred.
2. What are the lessons you learned? Write them down.
3. What changes can you make based on these lessons? Write them down.

Inspirational Thought

Every thought we have has the *potential* to change us.
Every action we take has the *potential* to change the world. We do have power and with that power comes responsibility.

Diva Pookie Boop

Diva Pookie Boop

Solution 33: Hope for a Good Outcome, but take Reasonable Precautions

When planning a vacation, you think about the things you would like to do, and the places you want to see. You hope for perfect weather and pray for a safe trip. You are hoping for a good outcome.

However, it wouldn't hurt to prepare for the worst by packing an umbrella, taking a jacket, checking the tread on the tires, filling the car with gas. In addition, take a map, just in case there are road construction detours or the GPS gets confused and keeps repeating, *"recalculating."*

My in-laws drove out of state to attend a funeral. They had a flat tire. When they replaced the tire with the spare, it was flat too. This caused much stress and a long delay. They didn't take reasonable precautions.

Several weeks later when we set off for a family reunion, I asked my husband to check my spare tire and indeed, it was low on air. We filled it and packed our portable inflation device that runs off the internal plug-in socket. We didn't have any problems, but it gave me peace of mind to know we were prepared. I generally try to learn from other people's mistakes and mishaps. If you are wise, you will, too.

> **Hope and plan for the best in your life, but also buy insurance, have an emergency fund, and start saving for your retirement NOW!**

Hope and plan for the best in your life, but also buy insurance, have an emergency fund, and start saving for your retirement, NOW! Did you realize that if you accumulate money for your retirement by saving ten to twenty percent of any monetary gifts or earnings that you acquire your whole life, and place that savings in a safe investment and keep it there, you could be a millionaire by the time you retire? Social Security may not be in existence by the time you retire, so it's best to prepare for your future. Being prepared reduces anxiety, worry, and future hardships.

> **Being prepared reduces anxiety, worry, and future hardships.**

Positive Direction Intervention

1. Check your car. Do you have jumper cables, a flashlight, water, energy bars, a blanket, a spare tire that is inflated, and tools to change the tire, a screwdriver, and a portable tire inflator? Include a candle, for light and warmth during a snowstorm.
2. At home, do you have fire extinguishers, smoke detectors, and secure locks for your doors?
3. If you're a parent, have you taken a CPR class for children and a first-aid course?
4. If you have a computer, do you have Internet security software, keep it updated, and have good passwords?
5. Are you saving every month for your retirement? Start small if necessary, but start.

Inspirational Thought

Diva Pookie Boop

Diva Pookie Boop

Solution 34: Have Plan "A", Plan "B" and Plan "C"

Robert Burns wrote in the poem "To a Mouse" in 1785, "The best laid schemes of mice and men go often askew." No matter how hard you try, you cannot possibly think of every contributing factor to a situation. Think ahead and have another plan prepared in case your first plan is not successful.

Thomas Edison used many different approaches before he succeeded in inventing the light bulb. He kept trying until he got it right, because he always had his next approach in mind.

> **Think ahead and have another plan prepared in case your first plan is not successful.**

A psychiatrist I worked with and admired, always made the last few sentences he dictated about a patient's treatment regime, his next plan to resolve the patient's problem. He knew that people are unique and what works for one patient may not work for another.

As a professional speaker, I always have an alternative plan. Recently at a conference my equipment for some reason didn't work with the facility's projector. My Plan B was to try my own projector that I brought as a backup. Thank goodness it worked and I didn't have to go to Plan C.

The other advantage of this approach is that back-up plans will help you feel less discouraged if your initial plan doesn't work. Less discouragement means more happiness.

Positive Direction Intervention

The next time you plan an approach to a problem, think about your back up plan, too. It will help things go smoother if the first idea doesn't work out perfectly. This will help you feel more confident.

Inspirational Thought

Fear is a monster that feeds off of your emotions - draining you of your confidence. Fear is not only a parasite, it is a thief that steals your dreams and your future. If you aren't careful, fear will make you a prisoner in your own mind.

Diva Pookie Boop

Diva Pookie Boop

Solution 35: "This Too Shall Pass"

"This too shall pass" originated from Persian Sufi poets. King Solomon and President Abraham Lincoln often used this phrase. Change is a constant; every day offers a new opportunity.

It may feel as if a painful situation will go on forever, but everything eventually ends. Concentrate on what you want the outcome to be.

> **Change is a constant; every day offers a new opportunity.**

Focus on your plans and goals for the future. Situations have a very strange way of turning around.

I remember the last days when my dad was dying of lung cancer due to smoking. At the end, there was nothing to do but try to keep him comfortable. Every day was full of bittersweet anguish, that seemed as if it would go on forever. I would pray and ask God to offer something positive each day to help me survive that sad ordeal. Each day something lifted my spirits and helped me to stay strong for my dad. Once it was a beautiful sunset and another time someone brought me a home cooked meal to the hospital. There were many small things and kind gestures, which sustained me. Once I was driving along when I spotted a store selling outdoor furniture. In front of the store, on display, was a table and chairs with a tropical, hot pink umbrella and cushions. It was surrounded by hundreds of plastic pink flamingos. I laughed so hard I had to pull off the road. It's amazing how small things can shift our moods to a positive place.

Eventually my father passed and left behind his suffering. That day ended my agony too, because I no longer had to helplessly watch his struggle. I learned a great deal about love, perseverance, and letting go.

"The one constant is change" was a famous quote by Heraclitus, who was a Greek philosopher. When you have a bad day, remember, "This too shall pass."

Positive Direction Intervention

Every time you feel an urge to do something you shouldn't do or think a bad situation will go on forever remember, "This too shall pass." I've had many recovering patient's report that delaying the gratification of an urge to relapse on alcohol, drugs, or sweets, allowed the urge to pass.

Inspirational Thought

Diva Pookie Boop

Diva Pookie Boop

Solution 36: Change Is Inevitable

Change happens constantly. To attempt to stop or resist change is a waster of time and effort. Instead, embrace change, and make it work for you.

1. Change is necessary and unavoidable. Trying to avoid it can cause you to be unhappy.
2. Find something positive in every new situation. By focusing on the positives, transition is easier. Better to think *this is my opportunity to meet new friends* than *I don't know anyone here.*
3. Guard your attitude from negative people by avoiding them if possible. Negativity breeds unhappiness.
4. Life is about progress, not perfection. Acknowledge your small victories to yourself and others.
5. It is difficult to move forward into the future, while you're dragging the past behind you. Hoarding negative emotions only slows you down and makes you unhappy.
6. Remember, whatever we resist keeps happening until we stop resisting. Accept what you can't change.
7. Happiness is a state of mind that resides inside you, so you choose your emotional state.
8. Establish a support system as soon as possible. Support lifts you and reduces your burden.
9. Acceptance is the key to serenity.

10. Most important: it is not what happens to you, but what you make of the situation that matters. You and you alone, determine the impact an event has on you and your life.

When I first moved to North Alabama from my home town of Birmingham, I wasn't embracing change. I took every opportunity to ignore all the positive aspects of my new home. On every occasion possible, I would compare my new home to Birmingham in a negative way. I didn't realize I had fallen into this destructive trap, until I was in the waiting room of a doctor's office. I was expounding to a fellow patient that Birmingham was much better than this area. Little did I know that this lady was a native of the area who loved her hometown, just as I loved mine. She graciously listened to me for twenty or so minutes.

> **Embrace change and make it work for you!**

A true Southerner, she politely told me, "We do *not* take hostages. If you are unhappy here you should go back to Birmingham."

When I finally closed my gaping mouth, I apologized to her. I knew she was right. I was responsible for my own unhappiness and discontent.

> **Hoarding negative emotions only slows you down and makes you unhappy.**

I have grown to love where I live. If given an opportunity to move back to Birmingham, I would have to pass. This is now my home. Embrace change and make it work for you, too.

Positive Direction Intervention

1. Are you making yourself miserable by clinging to the past or old procedures?
2. Think of a current situation in which you need to embrace change. Walk right up to that Change Monster, kiss it on the nose, and give it a big hug.

Diva Pookie Boop

Solution 37: Avoid Primary and Secondary Abuse

Mary, a new client, recounted the domestic violence incident that accounted for her black eye. This wasn't the first incident of abuse. Mary had previously left her unfaithful, controlling, jealous, and abusive husband four times, but always returned with her children.

The national average is *seven!* Women and men in abusive situations return to their abusers an average of seven times, before they get out of the Black Hole and choose to leave for good.

I was concerned for Mary and her children, so I asked, "Did your children witness this incident?"

"They were in the bedroom for most of it, but they came out when he started hitting me. My oldest called 911."

"Mary, you can decide to live in abuse, but your children don't have a choice. You make that decision for them."

"He has never laid a hand on my kids." Mary's indignant expression and folded arms sent a message of resistance. "I would never let a man hurt my kids!"

Abuse can be verbal, emotional, economical, physical or sexual.

Mary did let her husband hurt her children. She didn't understand that her husband was psychologically damaging the children. She was letting this man damage her children emotionally on a daily basis. This type of abuse is "secondary abuse," the abuse a witness endures when watching cruel acts. Mary had no idea what normal society considered abuse. This was because she lived in abuse her entire life; abuse was normal. Abuse can be verbal, emotional, economical, physical, or sexual.

The following are some examples of verbal abuse:
- Name-calling
- Cursing at someone
- Screaming

Examples of emotional abuse are:
- Intimidation
- Threats
- Put-downs
- Taunts

The following are examples of economical abuse:
- Not allowing a person to earn an income
- Complete control of the finances
- Hiding money

Examples of physical abuse are:
- Constraint
- Pushing
- Pinching
- Slapping
- Punching
- Kicking
- Hair pulling

- Choking
- Burning someone

The following are examples of sexual abuse:
- Unsolicited touching or fondling
- Forced sexual activity
- Sexual activity with minors

These are just a few examples; the list is much longer. Mary was involved in primary abuse. She personally received the abuse. The secondary abuse was what happened to her children. They experienced the sights and sounds of abuse. Both Mary and her children experienced the fear and the physiological "fight or flight" response at the time of the abuse. They all lived the abuse cycle. Each day they scanned their abuser for signals of danger, adjusted their behavior, and cautiously proceeded through day-to-day life. No person deserves abuse, primary or secondary.

> **No person deserves abuse, primary or secondary.**

According to a study done by the CDC in 2011, "On average, 24 people per minute are victims of rape, physical violence, or stalking by an intimate partner in the United States. Over the course of a year, that equals more than 12 million women and men." Safety is a primary concern. Every human deserves to feel safe.

> **Safety is a primary concern. Every human deserves to feel safe.**

Don't become a statistic. If you are in an abusive situation, seek safety. There is probably a shelter in your area. Do something before it's too late.

Mary didn't listen. She didn't protect herself or her children. The next day another violent episode occurred. Mary's husband hit her oldest child when she tried to stop the skirmish. An ambulance transported Mary and her daughter to the hospital where their injuries were treated. The county social workers, who were already invesigating this family, took custody of the children. They were placed in foster care. Arrangements were made for counseling to help the children deal with their secondary abuse issues. Unfortunately, they were placed into different foster homes. The police arrested the perpetrator for domestic violence and child abuse.

It took Mary one year to regain custody of her children and another six months before her case was closed. I would love to be able to report that I didn't see this happen dozens of times over the years, but I did.

Mary and her children suffered, because as a mother, she wouldn't make the decision and take the action necessary to keep her and her children safe. Please don't make the same mistake. Feeling unsafe can steal your fleeting moments of happiness.

Positive Direction Intervention

1. Take precautions to be safe every day of your life. I am not advocating that you live in fear, just that you take healthy precautions. Lock your doors, scan the area before walking to your car with your key in hand, and buckle your safety belt.
2. If you are living in abuse, get help. Find a shelter in your area, plan carefully, and when safe to do so, move to safety. You deserve to be safe.

Inspirational Thought

Red is my power color. Light blue makes me feel calm. Yellow lifts my spirits. Decide what colors help you feel better and wear them as you need them.

Diva Pookie Boop

Diva Pookie Boop

Solution 38: Take Out Your Personal Garbage

Like the rest of humanity, you probably have a pile of personal emotional garbage. It's similar to regular garbage, which stinks, clutters life, and can carry disease. The problem with emotional garbage is you can't see it, however, it's very real.

> **Your toxic emotions actually poison you from the inside.**

Mary, described in the previous chapter had collected a great deal of emotional garbage while living with her abusive husband. She collected even more from the fru-stration she felt about the foster care system and the loss of her children. All this made a heavy burden for her to bear and she developed a number of stress-related physical problems.

Toxic emotions may be the number one contributing factor to many of the world's major health problems today. Your toxic emotions actually poison you from the inside.

> **All of the negative thoughts and emotions you hoard produce an energy-sapping burden on your life.**

Negative emotions and stress release harmful amounts of cortisol and adrenaline into your body. Anger, anxiety, and depression interfere with your immune system and its fight to protect your body.

Emotional garbage is also a heavy burden on your unconscious mind. Imagine if you picked up a stone to match the size of each of your negative emotions, labeled it, and put it in a backpack. If you wore that backpack all day, every day, how much would you accomplish? All of the negative thoughts and emotions you hoard produce an energy-sapping burden on your life. Empty your emotional garbage on a regular basis and see how much more you can accomplish.

Positive Direction Intervention

Make a list of all the people who have hurt you in your life. Congratulations, you have just identified part of your emotional garbage.

Inspirational Thought

Be mindful and in the moment. Focus on where you are, who you are with, and what you are doing. Don't let the distractions of life steal your focus.

Diva Pookie Boop

Diva Pookie Boop

Solution 39: Use Forgiveness as Your Shovel

You are probably aware of your need to eliminate your emotional trash, but unsure of the best method of disposal. Garbage trucks don't travel around your community to collect your emotional trash. Telephone books don't list emotional dumpsites. So how do you get rid of this mess?

Use forgiveness as your personal shovel. Deep unconscious forgiveness is the only way to rid yourself of negative emotions. How-ever, there is some basic knowledge that you must first know.

> **The past provides us with insight, fond memories, personal growth, and valuable lessons. Forgive the rest and move forward with your life.**

1. Forgiveness is about you, not the other person. The offending party doesn't have to know that you've forgiven them or to even be alive for that matter.

2. Forgiveness doesn't excuse the wrongdoing and doesn't make it right. A wrongful deed will remain wrong.

3. Forgiveness doesn't mean that the wrongful deed didn't happen. It happened, but will be relegated to the past, instead of residing in today.

4. Forgiveness cleanses you, which allows more space for positive, growth-enhancing thoughts, feelings, and behaviors.

5. Forgiveness saves you from victimhood. Victimhood is the equivalent of wearing a flashing sign that advertises two alternating messages: *Use Me* and *Hurt Me*.

6. Anger and resentment do not protect you from hurt, but instead wall you in with those toxic emotions. This shield of resentment also blocks positive people from your life, because you are unable to trust people and your own judgment. Self-confidence and good self-esteem are your best protection.

7. Forgiveness sets you up for positive cause and effect. Hence the proverb, "What goes around comes around."

The past provides us with insight, fond memories, personal growth, and valuable lessons. Forgive the rest and move forward with your life.

This is a process, which may require a mental health professional. Don't believe the stereotypes. Contrary to popular belief, only a select number of mental health professionals deal with biologically-based mental illnesses. Many counselors, psychologists, family therapists, social workers, and pastoral counselors work with the

> **Use forgiveness as a shovel**

walking wounded, who are in a quest to eliminate emotional garbage.

Positive Direction Intervention

Make the choice to change your future and remove other people's power and control over your life through forgiveness. If you don't know how, find someone to help you. The exact details are beyond the scope of this book.

Diva Pookie Boop

Solution 40: Worry Less and Act More

Worry is a waste of time. Remember time is your most precious possession, the one you can't replace. Worry is not preventative maintenance; it doesn't stop anything from happening.

There is an old Swedish proverb: "Worry makes a big shadow of a small thing." It's true, because worry creates the worst-case scenario of an event in your mind and tortures you with your own self-created visions of that event.

> **Worry is not preventative maintenance; it doesn't stop anything from happening.**

Worry is also an ineffective way to express concern regarding a person or situation. If you look up the word "love" in the dictionary, worry is not included in the definition. Worry is also a lack of faith in God. If you believe that all things outside of your control are in God's care, why worry?

> **Worry is a lack of faith in God**

Many of my patients tell me they "prayed and put the situation in God's hands." Two minutes later, they tell me how worried they are about the situation, but don't realize their worry pulls it back in their hands.

Control over life consists of three categories:

1. People or situations over which we have control (Yourself),
2. People or situations over which we have influence (Other people, situations, and nature),
3. People or situations that are totally out of our control (Other people, situations, and nature).

If you have control over something, it is important to seek wise advice, prepare carefully, and take action. Doing something always feels better than inaction. However, don't fall prey to impatience. Timing is crucial.

If you have influence, offer your ideas, insights, or opinions in appropriate, non-violent ways. It is necessary to release the outcome of a situation if the other party isn't willing to listen. If you can't or shouldn't endure the situation (abuse), find a safe, responsible way to leave.

In situations where you have no control, I find prayer and placing the situation in God's hands to be the most helpful thing for me. However, God gave humans free will, which means we can choose to make poor choices despite excellent guidance.

Don't waste time with worry when you have the options to either take action or let go.

Positive Direction Intervention

1. Identify a situation over which you have no control. Write it down on paper, say a prayer to put it in God's hands, and then put the paper into your God Box. A God Box is any container that you have written "God Box" or "Higher Power" across the top. If you have trouble with the word "God", write Out of My Control" on top of the box.
2. If something comes up and you start to worry, take the paper out of the God Box or Out of My Control Box, say another prayer, and put it back in the box.

Diva Pookie Boop

Solution 41: Have Good Boundaries

Boundaries are the foundation of healthy human relations and are a demonstration of respect for everyone. Drama and conflict usually follow a boundary violation. Good boundaries are a way to prevent the building of resentments.

Here are a few examples of boundary violations:

1. To be unfaithful in an exclusive relationship.
2. To flirt or try to intervene into an exclusive relationship between two people.
3. To take or borrow objects without permission.
4. Don't search another person's property without his or her permission (Parents are encouraged to respect this, but legally they have a right to intervene in a child's life up to a certain age.)
5. To interject yourself into another person's business, problems, or arguments without his or her permission.

The list could be endless. There is some wisdom in the saying by Robert Frost, "Fences make good neighbors." Fences are a physical manifestation of the behavioral boundaries we should respect.

Marty and Jessica sat on my sofa, arms folded and legs crossed away from each other. Jessica, who was sobbing, uncrossed her arms to pull tissues from a box on my end table.

"She has been checking my email and my phone. I have no privacy," Marty said.

"I wouldn't have to check his phone if he hadn't been screwing around with that woman," Jessica said.

"That was months ago, when are you going to trust me?"

> **Drama and conflict usually follow a boundary violation. Good boundaries are a way to prevent the building of resentments.**

Unfortunately, I have heard these accusations before. One boundary violation begets another violation. The outcome is more hurt and distrust. It is best to respect boundaries and maintain trust with others in all we do. Behave in a manner that instills trust.

Positive Direction Intervention

There are a number of books in your public library, local book store, or advertised on the Internet related to boundaries and assertiveness. "Boundary Power: How I Treat You, How I Let You Treat Me, and How I Treat Myself" by Mike S. O'Neil and Charles E. Newbold is a good choice. Another is "Boundaries" by Dr. Henry Cloud and Dr. John Townsend. This one is a good pick if you are seeking a Christian focus. Find one that suits your needs and educate yourself about this topic.

Inspirational Thought

Diva Pookie Boop

Diva Pookie Boop

Solution 42: "No" is a Positive Word

Proper boundaries teach other people how to treat you. When you tell others, *"I don't care"* and *"Whatever,"* you are saying you lack an opinion, therefore, they are free to violate your boundaries. In the same vein, you unintentionally say "yes" through silence or by avoiding the word "no." "No" is a powerful positive word.

> **"No" is a powerful positive word.**

Unfortunately, people are reluctant to use it, because many perceive it as harsh. A gentler, kinder way to say no is, "I don't think so" or "Maybe some other time." Try it!

"No" is a boundary word. Good boundaries go both ways. Don't overstep into someone else's business and don't let them step into yours. Advice and opinions are best offered at the request of the re-ceiver, not spread like seeds at spring planting.

> **Boundaries express who you are as a person, as well as your likes and dislikes.**

Boundaries and the word "no", express who you are as a person, as well as your likes and dislikes. If you aren't clear about your preferences, you will have a harder time saying "no". A perfect example, is the heroine in a block buster movie, that exhibited a number of boundary issues and commitment phobia. Realization about her lack of boundaries and inability to say "no", hit when she discovered that she didn't even know how she liked her eggs cooked. Learn what you like and dislike.

People with good boundaries don't spread their personal and private business like seeds in the wind, but trust it to a few carefully chosen friends. You teach people how to treat you by what you let others say and do to you, and the limits you use in distributing your personal information.

> **You teach people how to treat you by what you let others say and do to you, and the limits you use in distributing your personal information.**

Years ago, when I was moving into a house, my next door neighbor came over to meet me and to check out my furniture. She told me a great deal of personal information about her family, including how much her house cost and the amount of her house payment. I learned in fifteen minutes from this person with poor boundaries, what would take months to learn in a healthy friendship.

Then she asked me, "How much is your house payment?"

I evasively responded, "The same as the last one."

She didn't pursue the question, but if she had, I would have responded, "That is personal information."

Poor boundaries and avoiding the word, "no", can lead to deep and long-held resentments. Resentment isn't a happy emotion.

Positive Direction Intervention

1. Are your actions saying *respect me* or *abuse me*?
2. Are you sharing too much information too soon?

3. What are you blogging and placing on social media sites for complete strangers to know about your personal life?
4. Are you sharing personal information with untrustworthy people? If so, CHANGE IT NOW!

Inspirational Thought

I accept and love all aspects of myself. I'm NOT perfect, because I am a cat. It is my imperfections that make me lovable. Perfect cats (and people) are intimidating.

Diva Pookie Boop

Diva Pookie Boop

Solution 43: You Can Detach in a Loving Way

To detach means to separate yourself in a healthy way from negative situations over which you have no control. It doesn't mean you stop caring about people or outcomes. It is learning the difference between *enabling* others to continue bad behavior, versus *helping* people to learn, grow, and reach their true potential. You hurt people by stealing their consequences.

When someone steals a consequence by removing it, he or she becomes a life-lesson thief, and sets the stage for a repetitive cycle of wrongful actions. People learn from both positive and negative consequences.

There is a difference between *caring* about others and *taking care of them*. Detachment isn't about "fixing" people or situations, but encouraging and supporting people while they correct their own problems and mistakes. It's not necessary for you to be in the middle of everyone's life providing direction, advice, and a rescue operation. In general, people need to face reality, search out their own solutions, and affect their own destiny in life.

> **People learn from both positive and negative consequences.**

As with all of life, there are exceptions. If a person is under the legal care of another (for example a minor or disabled person), then the caretaker has moral and legal responsibilities, but even then, should not steal consequences and learning experiences. If you are personally responsible for placing someone into a situation that caused harm, you need to help clean up any negative consequences of your actions.

> **The harsh reality is, there may not always be someone around to rescue you or the ones you love. Self-sufficiency is important.**

One of my colleagues shared that her husband bought her a mug with the message: "Resign as General Manager of the Universe." I can relate, because a good friend of mine told me to rip the "Master of the Universe patch off of my sleeve." The harsh reality is, there may not always be someone around to rescue you or the ones you love. Self-sufficiency is important.

Becoming caught up in other people's drama is a great way to stay unhappy, so avoid it if possible.

Positive Direction Intervention

1. Identify a situation or person from whom you need to detach.
2. Are you having trouble detaching because you like to feel needed? If so, there are healthier ways to find your purpose in life.
3. Practice detachment. You may only be successful for short periods at first, but you will get the hang of it. A life skill requires persistent practice.

Inspirational Thought

Diva Pookie Boop

Diva Pookie Boop

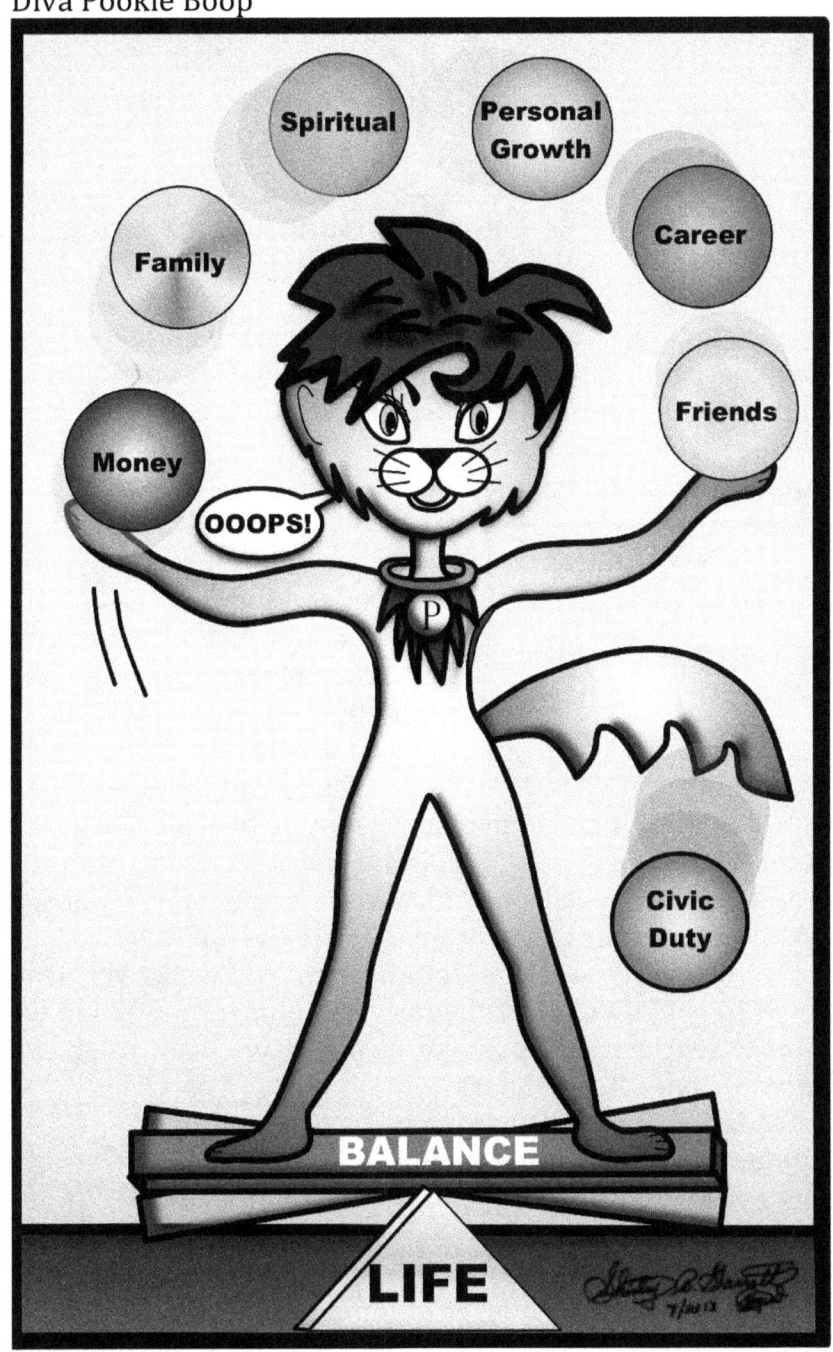

Solution 44: Balance, Balance, Balance

An unbalanced life is a major contributor to unhappiness and disease. The body and psyche function best under conditions of homeostasis, which is structure and balance. Too much of anything is a bad thing and can turn your life topsy-turvy

> **Too much of anything is a bad thing and can turn your life topsy-turvy.**

Moderation creates less stress on you, emotionally and physically. Moderation doesn't mean the absence of adventure or fun. Moderation is the avoidance of self- or other-induced drama.

There will be times when you will intentionally unbalance your life to achieve a goal. I recently watched a man riding a unicycle. Every time he wanted to move, he leaned forward to create an unbalanced position to get the momentum to move the unicycle.

We do the same thing when we walk. We lean forward slightly to start the forward momentum. When we stop to rest or reassess what direction we want to go, we spread our feet apart to provide balance. When we pursue a goal, we intentionally move ourselves out of balance to gain momentum, and then we return to a more balanced

> **Avoid drama-addicted people if possible.**

state to let things settle. It is important to moderate this intentional imbalanced state, by not staying out of balance too long.

There will always be naturally occurring drama in life, commonly referred to as crisis. However, avoid drama-addicted people if possible. If there is no crisis, the drama addict will create one over small, simple issues. If there is an emotional pot to stir, the drama addict will whip it into frenzy. If there is a genuine crisis, a drama addict will escalate it into an earth-shattering event. I once had a patient tell me his drama-addicted girlfriend left him feeling as if he was living in a natural disaster. A drama addict is a living, walking, talking, tornado, hurricane, earthquake, and wildfire combined.

> **A drama addict is a living, walking, talking, tornado, hurricane, earthquake, and wildfire combined.**

If you are known as a "Drama Queen" or "Drama King," it is best to change that pattern now. If you don't, you are setting yourself up for a life of unhappiness, relationship problems, employment issues, health con-cerns, and a shortened lifespan. Drama addiction typically comes from self-centeredness, emotional damage, fear, and pride. If you are a drama addict, your concerns are likely to be ignored and dis-counted with a *"Here she (he) goes again"* attitude. You will not be respected or taken seriously as a person. Generally, happiness doesn't exist in high-drama environments, but misery does.

> **There will be times when you will intentionally unbalance your life to achieve a goal.**

My dad often quoted, "Don't make a mountain out of a molehill," from Henry Ellis and "Give each problem its due." This is wise advice to follow.

Positive Direction Intervention

1. If you're involved with a drama addict, consider whether it is wise to continue the friendship. Is this a healthy relationship for you? Is this person disturbing your peace of mind and balance?
2. If it is a family member, for your mental health do you need to control the frequency and duration of your contact with that relative?
3. If you are a drama addict, please seek help to change the patterns of thoughts and behaviors that will keep you circling the Black Hole of misery.

Diva Pookie Boop

Solution 45: Be a Thermostat, Not a Thermometer

A thermometer is a device that measures and records the temperature of the atmosphere or surroundings and then moves to match it. Young children are emotional thermometers who adjust to their environment. When a mother or father starts to yell in the presence of a child, that child generally becomes upset as well. Drama addicts respond like thermometers, because they have not learned to regulate their emotional responses to the world around them.

> **Drama addicts respond like thermometers, because they have not learned to regulate their emotional responses to the world around them.**

A thermostat is a device that measures the temperature of the environment and then responds in an effective way to regulate and provide balance. If a thermostat is set at sixty-eight degrees and the atmosphere warms or cools significantly, the heating or cooling unit turns on to bring the room back into balance. Mature adults and wise teens learn to become self-regulating thermostats. When other people whip up a little drama or events escalate into a crisis, mature and balanced people do the following:

1. Acknowledge the situation ("I can see you are upset, and I am willing to listen."),
2. Ask themselves some questions ("What is *really* going on here?"),
3. Calm down and regain emotional control deep breath or time-out by leaving the room to calm down,
4. Set appropriate boundaries ("If you don't stop yelling and calling me names, I will have to leave until you calm down."),
5. Ask for help when necessary (Call 911).

People who are thermometers spend their whole lives controlled by the emotions, actions, whims, and the drama of others.

People who mature into thermostats learn to self-regulate their emotional states and control the impact people and situations have on their emotional or physical well-being.

Positive Direction Intervention

1. Are you a thermostat or a thermometer?
2. Practice the steps above to regulate your emotions and set good boundaries. Practice. Don't worry if you don't get it exactly right. Keep trying.
3. Buy a tiny level at the hardware store and use it as a physical reminder to keep your bubble in the middle, in order to keep things level in your life.

Inspirational Thought

Diva Pookie Boop

Diva Pookie Boop

Solution 46: Control Your Mouth

Words are a powerful force. They have the capability to influence people in a positive or negative way. Whoever wrote the old folk saying, "Sticks and stones may break my bones, but words will never hurt me," was **WRONG**!

When I was a child, I was very thin and wore glasses. My first year at a new school, my classmates verbally and emotionally bullied me almost every day. Sometimes I would go home in tears. My parents did their best to console me and often repeated, "Sticks and stones may break my bones, but words will never hurt me." One day I told my mother, "Why do you keep telling me that when it's not true? Words hurt!"

Choose your words wisely and think before you speak.

Words emotionally wound people. Hurtful words can drain con-fidence, lower self-esteem, and demoralize a person. Positive words can soothe, encourage, and motivate. The intensity of the words we use can raise us to great heights, drop us into despair, or send us out of control.

It is important to vary the intensity of the words we use to match the intensity of the situation. The word *irritated* elicits a much lower emotional response than the word *furious*. Choose your words wisely and think before you speak.

Say what you choose in your head, but edit it before it exits your mouth. Once you have spoken harsh words, the damage has been done, and those words can't be reclaimed. Remember, words have power, so choose them carefully.

Positive Direction Intervention

1. In the future, slow down and think before you speak. Speak to encourage and influence, not to harm. No sane person wants to cooperate when spoken to harshly. I know this is hard, because I had to overcome "Foot in Mouth Disease". If I can do it, so can you.
2. Who have you spoken to in a harsh way? Do you need to apologize?

Inspirational Thought

You are responsible for your own thoughts, decisions, and behaviors. When you blame others, you give them power over you and your destiny. Only by taking complete responsibility for where you are today, can you wield the power to move to the next level in your life.

Diva Pookie Boop

Diva Pookie Boop

Solution 47: Love More–Fear Less

When people respond out of fear they sometimes withdraw, attack (verbally or physically), shun others, are intolerant, or are unkind. Fears can be real (situations that *are* happening) or imagined (situations that *may* happen).

If you live your life based on fear, you will never truly experience life to its fullest.

There are risks that you should avoid because of the level of danger. However, if you don't take some risks, you may not have the career you want, a successful business, or find the ideal mate.

> **If you live your life based on fear, you will never truly experience life to its fullest.**

Most multi-millionaires take calculated risks. Conrad Hilton is a perfect example of a person who took a chance and made his Hilton Hotel chain a success. Hilton was one of eight children born to immigrants. He intended to purchase a bank, but instead, bought a hotel in 1919. He gradually built his empire, but nearly bankrupted during the great depression. He lost some of his hotels, but took some calculatd risks and made a post-depression comeback. Today Hilton is still a successful hotel chain. Like Conrad Hilton, many people don't succeed on the first or second try, but they analyze their mistakes, learn from them, and try again. A goal that doesn't result in one hundred percent success isn't failure, *it's learning.*

Failure is being too afraid to try in the first place. Imagine if a baby was too scared to walk, because he or she might fall down. What if the baby fell once and thought, "That's it. I fell down. I'm not going to try to walk again."

Courage is not the absence of fear. Courage is being afraid and trying anyway.

> **Courage is not the absence of fear. Courage is being afraid and trying anyway.**

Love and faith can calm our fears. When people act out of love, they are more open, kind, and generous. The Bible verse from 1 Corinthians 13:4-8 (NIV, 1984 edition) says it well:

> **A goal that doesn't result in one hundred percent success isn't failure, *it's learning.***

"Love is patient, love is kind. It does not envy, it does not boast, it is not proud. It is not rude, it is not self-seeking, it is not easily angered, it keeps no record of wrongs. Love does not delight in evil, but rejoices with the truth. It always protects, always trusts, always hopes, always perseveres. Love never fails."

If everyone loved each other to this standard, the world would be a kinder, gentler place to reside and there would be less fear.

Positive Direction Intervention

Put the Bible verse 1 Corinthians 13:4-8 where you can see it and be reminded to act out of love, not fear.

Inspirational Thought

Diva Pookie Boop

Diva Pookie Boop

Solution 48: Practice Tolerance

Tolerance is respect for people as human beings, even if you disagree and don't respect their opinions, beliefs, and behaviors. It is possible to disagree with a person and still care about that individual as a human being. The opposite of tolerance is to be judgmental or to shun.

There were numerous times while growing up, that I disappointed my father with my immature decisions and behaviors. He never judged me as a person. He made it clear he disapproved of my negative actions, but he still loved me as his daughter. That was a powerful teaching tool. It is healing to be able to recognize the light in people while they are standing in darkness. However, don't hop into the darkness with them!

> **It is healing to be able to recognize the light in people while they are standing in darkness. However, don't hop into the darkness with them!**

> **It is possible to disagree with a person's opinion or behaviors and still care about that individual as a human being.**

My favorite quote on this topic is, "Determine to be tender with the young, compassionate with the aged, sympathetic with the striving, and tolerant with the weak and wrong. Sometime in life you will have been all of these." Lloyd Shearer

Years ago I attended some music festivals and camped with some friends. One of the key couples, Mae and Jerry, always saw the best in everyone, even though each of us had our imperfections. They were very tolerant. The interesting thing I observed was that everyone always gave this couple their best behavior. Mae and Jerry made everyone feel accepted, special, and actually made us want to be better people.

Don't forget to be tolerant with yourself, as well. You are a creative masterpiece in progress, and you are learning and evolving every day.

Positive Direction Intervention

Think of at least three small changes for the better you have made in the last year. Write them down so you can see them. Now pat yourself on the back and commit to more changes that are positive.

Inspirational Thought

Knowledge is what we know. Wisdom is the knowledge that we use in our everyday lives. Be wise and use what you have learned. Keep using it everyday, so you don't forget what you have learned.

Diva Pookie Boop

Diva Pookie Boop

Solution 49: Recreate Yourself

Each day is a new opportunity to make the choice: Continue your current path in life or choose a different path to follow. Each day is an opportunity to change yourself and eventually the world! Create yourself into the person you want to be and create the life you want to live. I'm not asking you to do anything you haven't already been doing for years. Yes, you created the life you are living, through your decisions and choices. Therefore, you can create a different one, a happier one.

Imagine what would happen if people came together with one purpose, to heal themselves and the world of its woes. The world would change one person at a time.

Think of all the people who experience your moods, feelings, thoughts, and behaviors on a day-to-day basis at your home, school, workplace, and through the electronic media you use. Each one of those people has an effect on more people, who influence more people. Do the math; the possibilities are astounding! This is the *power of one*, and it can influence the world. You have the power to recreate yourself, to rewrite your life script.

> **You have the power to recreate yourself, to rewrite your life script.**

Just because your family gave you a life script as a child, doesn't mean you don't have the power and control to write your own, with the outcome you prefer. You are

NOT destined to repeat your parent's mistakes. If you do repeat them, it was *your* choice.

I could have chosen to repeat my mother's life, but I didn't. I chose a different life. I'm dedicating this poem to my mother.

If Only ...

Only now do I realize mother, that you were a prisoner in your own life.

The shackles of your fear, anxiety, and depression chained you to our family.

Your soul cried out to create and shine, as if you were a star destined to change the universe.

Your many talents remained unacknowledged and not encouraged.

You constantly sought attention in negative ways, striving to exist through drama and anger.

You told me to "never have children they will ruin your life."

I'm sure you felt as if we stole yours.

You never wanted a girl, because you feared I would live *your* life.

Your life was a path of disappointment that snaked its way through narrow dark hallways of depression and fear.

Instead, I live your dreams and aspirations. Every day I live the life you desired, craved, and deserved.

You watched in wonder as I waltzed my way through the world.

You expressed awe at my courage and perseverance.

I lived your dreams through my accomplishments and creativity.

I do many of the things that you wished you had the courage and the support to try.

I live my life differently, because I learned from your unhappiness. Thank you for teaching me those lessons.

Every day I perform magic by using the creativity from your genes to create something to help or inspire others.

This is my way to balance some of the negative impact you had on the world.

It is my gift to you for giving me life. That was the greatest gift you had to give.

If only... you had realized, that your children were your success.

> **You are NOT destined to repeat your parent's mistakes. If you do repeat them, it is *your* choice.**

Positive Direction Intervention

It's now time for you to recreate yourself and your life. Take paper and pen and write out the life you want to create. Be specific. Focus each day on these goals and make all your decisions and choices with these goals in mind. Do it now.

Stop the Craziness: Simple Life Solutions

Diva Pookie Boop

Solution 50: The Beginning!

You are an evolving and growing person, designed to fulfill your maximum potential. Humans are created equal, but not with the same abilities. Don't waste time comparing yourself to others. You are an authentic original. There is only one of you.

> **Don't waste time comparing yourself to others. You are an authentic original. There is only one of you.**

You can *choose* to reach your potential and have a happy life. Life is about choices. No one can make you do it or do it for you. You alone have the sole power to excel or royally screw up your life. There will be wise people available to teach and guide you throughout your life. Choose your mentors and friends carefully, so your focus stays true-to-course throughout your journey. Take some small positive action toward excellence every single day.

> **Take some small positive action toward excellence every single day.**

Set your direction wisely and make your preparations. Clean up your past mistakes, so they don't become future barriers. Do the right thing, for the right reasons, the right way.

I know you can do it. Why, you may ask? I changed my life by making better choices and daring to try my best. It's a daily choice and commitment for me. Anything one person has achieved, another can too.

> **Clean up your past mistakes, so they don't become future barriers.**

For over twenty-six years of working with my patients, I watched many of them *choose* to achieve the life they desired. The barrier has been broken and the way paved. Many times, our barriers aren't real; they are only in our minds.

For centuries, no one was able to break the four-

> **Many times, our barriers aren't real; they are only in our minds.**

minute mile while running. Many considered it impossible. Roger Bannister broke this barrier when he came in with a time of 3 minutes, 59.4 seconds. Since then, many people have achieved this goal in running. Why? Someone else did it. It was achievable. If others have transformed their lives, and created happiness, so can you.

Don't waste your time regretting the past or feeling

> **You can't live in today, if you have one foot planted in the regrets of the past and the other standing in fear about your future.**

guilty. There is no value in doing this; it is a waste of your energy. You can't live in today, if you have one foot planted in the regrets of the past and the other standing in fear about your future. Today is where you change your life.

Now you have part of the knowledge. Use the call out boxes in this book as easy reminders of some of the key

> **Today is where you change your life.**

points. Reread the book to keep you inspired and on track. If you choose to go further, the help is available. Crank up your desire. Persist every day toward your journey to greatness.

Every moment is a fresh start and a new beginning.
Move in a positive direction.
Walk in beauty.
Be in tune with yourself.
Go for it and remember
YOU are a force!

Notes

About the Author

Dr. Shirley B. Garrett, Psy.D, is an author and retired psychologist/counselor, as well as a professional speaker and artist. While practicing as a therapist, she worked twenty-six years in the areas of mental health and substance abuse. Her self–improvement, Quick Tips Series is available on Amazon.

Dr. Garrett also writes fictional novels under the name Shirley B. Garrett. She is the author of the Charlie Stone Crime Thriller Series (DEADLY COMPULSION, DEADLY LESSONS, and DEADLY OBSESSIONS). DEADLY LESSONS was a 2018 finalist for a Silver Falchion Award and DEADLY OBSESSION is a 2020 finalist for the same award. Note: This series is rated R for sex and violence.

Dr. Garrett also wrote the Phoenix O'Leary Chick Lit Series (HOT FLASH DIVAS, HOT FLASH DESIRES, and HOT FLASH DECISIONS).

She lives in Alabama with her husband, and her bibliocat, Pookie, who inspired the cartoons in this book.

Reviews on this book are appreciated on your blogs, on GoodReads.com, and on Amazon.

https://www.ShirleyBGarrett.com
Facebook.com/ShirleyBGarrett
Twitter.com/ShirleyBGarrett

www.ingramcontent.com/pod-product-compliance
Lightning Source LLC
Chambersburg PA
CBHW070656100426
42735CB00039B/2158